When the evolution of our technologies is raising new questions about "jobs" and "work," Sutrisna Harjanto's thoughtful exploration of the formation of vocation is timely because he not only addresses the significance of the college years but also distinctively sheds light on the transitional five–ten years post-college. His research and the conclusions he draws are a welcome cross-cultural contribution to our understanding of human development for today's world. Particularly those who are curious about what can be revealed through a Christian lens, this book sheds light on the experience of discerning "a calling" in ways that challenge easy assumptions about self, society, and the formation of faithfulness.

Sharon Daloz Parks
Senior Fellow, Whidbey Institute, Clinton, WA, USA
Author, *Big Questions, Worthy Dreams*

Sutrisna Harjanto has thoughtfully addressed an increasingly important topic for the worldwide church – vocational stewardship. By exploring the experiences of Indonesian Christians in various occupations, he has also significantly broadened and thickened the overall discussion. Specifically, Sutrisna has built on the work of noted scholars like Sherman, Garber, and Parks by identifying phases of vocational development. Readers should take special note of his admonition to nurture mentoring relationships embedded in caring communities of practice during the developmentally crucial young adult years. I am very grateful to Sutrisna for extending our theoretical and contextual understanding of vocational stewardship.

Donald Guthrie
Director, PhD in Educational Studies Program,
Trinity Evangelical Divinity School, Deerfield, IL, USA

Harjanto has taken great care in clarifying the stages of developing vocational stewardship using adult developmental frameworks from psychological theories and spiritual formation practices, applying them towards cultivating meaning, calling and service at the workplace for the everyday Christian. True to his Asian roots, he has also incorporated various modes of empowering relationships and empowering communities as a basis for vocational stewardship which are often missed by western authors and theologians. Whether you are a pastor, workplace leader, disciple-maker or mentor in the workplace, this is a must-read, with globally applicable concepts with a unique Indonesian flavour.

Timothy Liu
Senior Associate, Marketplace Ministry, Lausanne Movement
Director of Ministry, Marketplace Christian Network, Singapore

Vocation is integral, not incidental, to the mission of God, and in this book by Sutrisna Harjanto we are given a wonderfully rich study of what this means for the working world of Indonesia. Historically informed, theologically rooted, and sociologically attentive, he has offered an outstanding treatment of the challenges facing men and women with professional responsibilities in twenty-first-century Jakarta and beyond, bringing hard-won insights to bear that are as relevant in England and as they are in India, in Brazil as they are in Kenya. I hope that his work finds its way into visions and strategies all over the world, more faithfully and effectively forming the next generation for vocations that will be common grace for the common good, signposts of hope and truth, justice and mercy for everyone everywhere.

Steven Garber
Professor of Marketplace Theology and Leadership,
Regent College, Vancouver, BC, Canada
Author, *Visions of Vocation*

I praise God and welcome the publication of this very important book on vocational stewardship among Indonesian Christian professionals. Vocational stewardship is well acknowledged as a very important element of a holistic Christian life, and yet, it has minimal attention among the Christians and churches in Indonesia.

The research outcomes which are the core of this book, enable us to understand what should be the "developing stages of vocational stewardship" that would systematically prepare students to internalize and practice all necessary steps and stages in ensuring graduates are ready to serve with a clear calling, making an impact for Christ through their professional services.

Several groups which are taking part in campus ministries in Indonesia such as Perkantas, Navigators, Campus Crusade, and others, may not have the holistic approach as outlined in this book for preparing students to be ready to implement a biblically based and Christ-centered vocational stewardship in pursuing their calling from God, and serving meaningfully in their professions.

It is my hope and prayer that the recommended stages relating to the development of vocational stewardship of Christian professionals presented in this book, will become important to all the groups who are participating in campus ministries and churches in general. I pray and hope that this book will be a blessing to many readers and the churches for the glory of God.

Jonathan Parapak
Rector, Universitas Pelita Harapan, Indonesia
A founder of Perkantas, International Fellowship of
Evangelical Students in Indonesia

The Development of Vocational Stewardship among Indonesian Christian Professionals

Spiritual Formation for Marketplace Ministry

Sutrisna Harjanto

MONOGRAPHS

Published 2018 by Langham Monographs
An imprint of Langham Publishing
www.langhampublishing.org

Langham Publishing and its imprints are a ministry of Langham Partnership

Langham Partnership
PO Box 296, Carlisle, Cumbria CA3 9WZ, UK
www.langham.org

ISBNs:
978-1-78368-465-6 Print
978-1-78368-466-3 ePub
978-1-78368-467-0 Mobi
978-1-78368-468-7 PDF

British Library Cataloguing-in-Publication Data
A catalogue record for this book is available from the British Library

ISBN: 978-1-78368-465-6

Cover & Book Design: projectluz.com

Dedication

To my wife, Lily, with deep thanksgiving for your selfless and endless support throughout the doctoral journey. And to my colleagues, with deep appreciation for dedicating your lives to helping young people pursue God's calling in their lives.

Contents

List of Tables

List of Figures

Acknowledgements

This research is the fruit of a long learning journey of which I am deeply indebted to many along the way. First, I would like to thank Dr Miriam Charter, who opened the door for me into the PhD EDS program at Trinity, along with the Waybright scholarship. Many thanks to Dr Donald Guthrie for your tireless mentoring and kind friendship along the doctoral journey. Thank you for introducing me to the academic works and dynamics of the faith-at-work movement. Special thanks also to Dr Steve Garber for your warm welcome and insights that come from many years of experiences in the field of vocation. It's a privilege to have you as my reader.

My gratitude for many people who have contributed to the research process and the final production of this book. Many thanks to the participants in this study for allowing your wonderful life stories to be part of this research. My appreciation to the transcription team – Christy, Grace, and Khara – for your excellent job. I am also indebted to my wife, Lily, and my daughter, Laura, for your great help translating the portion of interview quotes into English. Thank you Taina and Tim Baldwin for your very helpful feedback. My appreciation to Ilene Foote and Margaret Ward for your great help with the grammatical editing, and Kris Ford for the Trinity format editing.

Special thanks to Dr Riad Kassis who introduced my work to Langham Literature, and to the Langham Publishing team who have provided the wonderful opportunity for my dissertation to be published as part of Langham Monograph series. Many thanks, especially to Peter Kwant, Vivian Doub, and your editing team for your invaluable guidance and hard work in polishing my dissertation to get ready for a publication as a book.

I am indebted to Dr Deborah Colwill, who, with Dr Donald Guthrie, has taught me more research skills. During my course work I also have had the honor of learning from Dr James Moore, Dr James Plueddemann, Dr Perry

Downs, Dr Peter Cha, Dr Robert Priest, Dr Tasha Chapman, and Dr Camile Bishop. My deep appreciation also to Dr Samuel Sidjabat, at Tiranus Bible Seminary, who introduced me to the academic field of Christian Education before I came to Trinity.

I would like to express my deep gratitude to Trinity International University through the Waybright scholarship donor, ScholarLeaders International, and to Perkantas (IFES in Indonesia) for the generous scholarships and financial support that enabled me to complete this program. Many thanks for colleagues and friends in Perkantas and Bandung Theological Seminary for your support, encouragement and prayer throughout my doctoral journey.

I am also grateful for my EDS colleagues for living as a community of learners and for the fellowship within and beyond the classroom. Thanks so much to Ruth Park, Tim Baldwin, Kags Ndethiu, Jane Cha, Tina Lau, Sarinah Lo, Carl Hettler, Sharon Falkenheimer, Paige Cunningham, Hae-Won Kim, Eunsung Kim, and many others.

My deep gratitude for the communities to which my family and I have been a part of during our stay in the USA. Kate Reed and the wonderful ISSO ministry of TIU, Trinity Chinese Fellowship with the wonderful help in our first year of adjustment, Village Church of Lincolnshire with the warm fellowship and wonderful ministry, and Mike Philips with the wonderful ministry of Kids on Campus that helped my kids to grow.

Finally, I believe wholeheartedly that God was the One who works behind these wonderful people and communities. Praise be to God!

Abstract

This qualitative research explored the development of vocational steward-ship among Indonesian Christian professionals. Twenty-eight participants were purposively selected from the populations of Christian professionals in Jakarta and three surrounding cities. Data was collected through a semi-structured interview. Theology of work, holistic mission, and formation related with developmental perspectives were key theories to frame the dis-cussion on the research findings.

The findings suggest that three robust dimensions of vocational steward-ship, calling, service, and the meaning of work, were developed through different phases in a lifetime process. Four phases of development iden-tified through this research were introductory, formative, transition, and generative. For a fruitful formation, Christian educators need to take into account the unique characteristics of each phase. Central to these phases is the formative phase that significantly impacts the rest of a person's vocational stewardship journey. Also needing special attention is a crucial transition that follows, the early phase of integrating faith into work life. For most participants, these two key phases took place in their emerging adulthood.

The study also finds two important resources for the development of vocational stewardship: networks of empowering relationships and empow-ering communities. This includes the crucial roles of mentor and mentor-ing community in the formative and transitional phases. To give fruitful support, Christian educators need to provide well-functioning networks of those resources, whether in the local church or parachurch ministry context. Attention also needs to be given to the types of support most suitable with the phase of vocational stewardship development of those who are targeted.

CHAPTER 1

Introduction

Background of the Study

Christian professionals, through their daily work, have an important role in God's mission to bring the foretastes of God's shalom in this world. This awareness is a part of the resurgent awareness that work is an inherent part of our humanity and that God's redemptive work in Christ encompasses the whole aspect of human life and human relationships.[1]

The resurgent awareness of the deeper meaning of work and its inherent connection with Christian faith is reflected in the increasing efforts to develop a robust theology of work in the past three decades. For this purpose, theologians across various Christian traditions have attempted to develop a theology of work from different angles, including the creation account, human as God's image, vocation, the curse of the fall, eschatology, the Spirit, the Triune God, and the kingdom.[2] Attempts to develop multiple lenses of a theology of work also have been approached from various church traditions, including Reformed, Pentecostal, Baptist, and Wesleyan.[3]

At the same time, efforts to integrate faith and work in practice are reflected in what David Miller called a faith and work movement. He claims that this movement that has grown since the mid-1980s is "a loosely networked group of individual and collective activity, reacting against the

---

1. Wright, *Mission of God's People*.

2. E.g. Ryken, *Work and Leisure*; Bakke, *Joy at Work*; Hardy, *Fabric*; Rifkin, *End of Work*; Volf, *Work in the Spirit*; Witherington III, *Work*.

3. Bolt, *Economic Shalom*; Self, *Flourishing Churches and Communities*; Brand, *Flourishing Faith*; Wright, *How God Makes the World a Better Place*.

church's lack of support for those called to a life in the marketplace, and whose common drive is a deep desire to live a holistic life with particular attention to the integration of faith and work."[4] Based on his research, Miller divides different approaches by individuals and groups to integrate faith at work into four main types. (1) Ethic Type: Those in this group try to apply biblical principles at the workplace on the three different levels of personal, corporate, and society. (2) Evangelism/Expression Type: Those in this group "view work and workplace primarily as a mission field for evangelizing or witnessing to coworkers and others with whom they come in contact, including customers and suppliers."[5] People in this type tend to neglect addressing structural ethical issues and social injustice. (3) Experience Type: This group's "primary means of integrating faith and work involves questions of vocation, calling, meaning, and purpose in and through their marketplace professions."[6] (4) Enrichment Type: They primarily integrate faith and work in a personal level and their inward nature, "focusing on issues like healing, prayer, meditation, consciousness, transformation, and self-actualization."[7] Miller contends that the ideal is for people to integrate all four types in their faith and work as "Everywhere Integrators."[8]

While his research is based mostly in a Christian faith context, Miller also suggests that the framework can be applied to other religious and philosophical traditions as well. In fact, as Miller indicates, the faith and work movement does not exclusively develop within Christian faith communities. In the field of management, faith and work integration increasingly gained more attention in theory, research and practice as early as the 1990s.[9] The popular usage of terms such as "workplace spirituality" or "spirituality and the workplace" suggests the intention of developing a more generic and inclusive nature of faith and work integration for various beliefs.[10]

---

4. Miller, *God at Work*, 21.

5. Miller, 132.

6. Miller, 135.

7. Miller, 137.

8. Miller, 139.

9. Neal, *Handbook of Faith*; Marques, Dhiman, and King, *Workplace and Spirituality*; Fry and Geigle, "Spirituality and Religion."

10. Neal, *Handbook of Faith*, 10.

More specific attempts to develop a connection between work and mission are reflected in the emergence of several marketplace mission movements. Rundle, in "Restoring the Role of Business in Mission," lists a summary of the distinction of each movement.

(1) Tentmaking: "often used to describe individual Christians who find employment in a cross-cultural context, taking jobs in schools, hospitals or business, etc." (2) Marketplace Ministry: "refers to parachurch organizations that disciple and coach Christian business professionals to be more effective witnesses in the workplace. Increasingly, the term 'Workplace Ministry' is being used instead, which broadens the focus to include all working professionals." (3) Business as Mission (BAM) "refers to business (often called 'Great Commission Companies' or 'Kingdom Business') that are created and managed specifically for the purpose of advancing the cause of Christ in less-reached and/or less-developed parts of the world." (4) Christian Microenterprise Development: "seeks to help the world's poorest people start and run successful, God-honoring businesses, often with the help of small loans."[11]

However, a closer look at these marketplace mission movements would reveal that most of these movements put their emphasis only in the first or second type of Miller's integration. For example, Amy Sherman's study of fifteen evangelical marketplace ministries, of which some of them bear the name "international," indicated that most of their activities fall only into Miller's Ethics or Evangelism type. Another research that she and her team conducted on twenty-three Christian professional societies also indicated that the majority of these professional societies were "more internally than externally focused."[12] None of the groups reflected the Everywhere Integrator type, which according to Sherman, is the closest to the idea of faith and work integration from a missional perspective.

Amy Sherman was helpful in bringing the conversation on work and mission to a personal level. She coined the term "vocational stewardship" to refer to faith and work integration from a missional perspective. She contends that the OT *tsaddiqim* (the righteous) (Prov 11:10) takes seriously all three

11. Rundle, "Restoring," 760–761.
12. Sherman, *Kingdom Calling*, 97.

dimensions of righteousness: vertical, internal, and social. They reflect what a biblical faith and work integration from a missional perspective would look like. She suggests four pathways to be a Christian *tsadiqqim* in the present day to fulfill the foretastes of God's kingdom: (1) bloom: promoting the kingdom in and through the person's daily work; (2) donate: volunteering vocational talent outside the person's day job; (3) invent: launching a new social enterprise; (4) invest: participating in the church's targeted initiative. Sherman also stresses that "bloom" is the "primary and most important avenue for deploying vocational power."[13] For the purpose of this research, Sherman's term of "vocational stewardship" and its fulfillment through a person's daily work will be utilized as a reference point.

Problem Statement

For vocational stewardship to thrive, Christian workers need to be equipped and supported by their faith community. Some literature suggested helpful ideas for formation or discipleship strategies that Christian faith communities can use.[14] However, research suggests that church members are not well-equipped by their church for this important task.[15] Furthermore, very little empirical research, including in the Majority World context, has been conducted to find out what kind of formation or discipleship process really matters for these Christian professionals in their journey to integrate their work into God's work in thought and practice. Therefore, this research was conducted as a small step to fill the huge gap in literature that hopefully would also provide necessary information for Christian educators in helping to equip Christian professionals in their vocational stewardship journey.

Purpose of the Study

The purpose of this study was to explore the personal development of vocational stewardship among Indonesian Christian professionals. A better understanding of the process and factors, which have significantly influenced

---

13. Sherman, 144.

14. Notably Sherman, *Kingdom Calling*; Liu, Preece, and Wong, "Marketplace Ministry."

15. E.g. Miller, *God at Work*; Wuthnow, *God and Mammon*; Knapp, "Bridging Christian Ethics."

these Christian professionals in connecting their daily work with God's work in thoughts and practice, could bring important insights to Christian educators and church leaders in their attempts to equip these professionals for their role in God's mission. The study was conducted through a basic qualitative research.[16]

Research Questions

This study was guided by the following research questions:

1. How do Indonesian Christian professionals describe their vocational stewardship?
2. How do Indonesian Christian professionals describe the significance of their college years for the development of their vocational stewardship?
3. How do Indonesian Christian professionals describe the personal development of vocational stewardship after their college years?

The Significance of the Study

Theoretical Significance

Given that there has been very little research done in this area, this study seeks to provide a better understanding of formational elements in the integration of faith, work, and mission.

This study explored the intersection among various aspects, including theology of work, theology of mission, faith at work in practice, formation, and developmental theories, in the non-western context. The result of this study will hopefully contribute to the literature on the theology of work and mission from an educational perspective.

Practical Significance

A better understanding of the process and factors which have significantly influenced Christian professionals in connecting their daily work with God's work would bring important insights for educational practice. The result of this study could be beneficial, particularly for Christian educators and church

---

16. Merriam, *Qualitative Research*, 22–24.

leaders whose tasks are to equip and support professionals in fulfilling God's mission through their work life and their whole life (Eph 4:11–12). These insights could be beneficial whether in the contexts of the local church, parachurch, or academia, both in Indonesia and in other places where the results are transferable.

Definition of Terms

Christian Professionals

The term Christian professional refers to university graduates who work in various kinds of occupations, whether as employees, independent professionals (doctor, lawyer), or entrepreneurs (business person). The intention of this study is not to exclude those who work in the full-time Christian ministry (such as pastors, evangelists, or traditional missionaries), but it will put more focus on those who work in "secular" professions, since they were those who have struggled the most to understand the meaning of their daily work within the context of God's eternal work. In terms of proportion, the "secular" professionals comprise the majority of God's people compared to those who work in full time Christian ministry.

Vocational Stewardship

Vocational stewardship refers to the term proposed by Amy Sherman in her book *Kingdom Calling: Vocational Stewardship for the Common Good*. Here vocational stewardship is to be understood as "the intentional and strategic deployment of our vocational power – knowledge, platform, networks, position, influence, skills and reputation – to advance foretastes of God's kingdom."[17] While Christian hope refers to the full restoration of this world under God's rule at the eschaton (end of time), it is believed to be a Christian duty to bring the foretastes of grace, love, and justice, among other values of the kingdom to come.

---

17. Sherman, *Kingdom Calling*, 20.

God's Mission

God's mission in this study refers to what Peskett and Ramachandra argue, that mission is primarily God's activity.[18] "God is reaching out to his world through Christ and his Spirit. He is engaged in liberating the cosmos and humankind from its captivity to evil, and it is his purpose to gather the whole creation under the Lordship of Christ." Similarly, Wright also asserts that God has a mission, a purpose, and a goal for his whole creation.[19] His mission is what Paul called the "whole will of God" (Acts 20:27 cf. Eph 1:9–10), and God has called his People to participate in the fulfillment of that mission.

Development of Vocational Stewardship

The development of vocational stewardship in this study refers to the personal development of a sense of calling in one's work life, including both perception and action. My assumption is that despite some common characteristics which could be potentially identified, this development is unique for each person, according to his or her own unique life trajectories. The understanding of personal development being investigated in this study is not similar to the psychological understanding of developmental stages in human life, in which there has been a predetermined potentiality to be unfolded.[20] However, this study also attempted to find out whether there is any connection between the personal development of vocational stewardship and the theories of developmental stages.

---

18. Peskett and Ramachandra, *Message of Mission*, 29.
19. Wright, *Mission of God's People*, 24.
20. Merriam and Bierema, *Adult Learning*, 49.

CHAPTER 2

Precedent Literature

This chapter will provide an overview of various efforts to integrate faith, work, and mission – in theory and practice. Literature on the theology of work, theology of mission, and various types of related movements will be explored to provide an overview of attempts to connect Christian faith, human work, and God's mission. This chapter will also provide precedent literature about spiritual formation through a developmental lens, with the focus on the development of vocational stewardship in emerging adulthood.

Theology of Work

Darrell Cosden classifies various contemporary writings on work into three different types of literature: (1) theological reflections on work as a part of more comprehensive theological treatises in a systematic theology, (2) focused studies on work in which the nature and meaning of work becomes the main question in developing a more comprehensive Christian picture of work, and (3) ethical or contextual studies in which theological reflections on work are conducted while exploring pressing ethical issues related to work such as unemployment, discrimination at work, and exploitation of nature.[1] For the purpose of this study, the second type will become the focus, since this type is the one that has the most potential to contribute significantly to our understanding of work from the biblical perspective, and hence to find the connection between work and mission on the foundational level.

The emergence of theology of work as a concept is quite a recent development, even though theological reflections on work can be traced back

---

1. Cosden, *Theology of Work*.

throughout centuries to biblical times. The emergence of this concept after the Second World War was largely the result of French Catholic theologians' attempts to develop a theology of "secular realities."[2] This new approach has become an important starting point in a comprehensive theological study of the nature and meaning of work.

Cosden argues that "the normative theological understanding of work is best construed threefold as a dynamic interrelationship of instrumental, relational, and ontological aspects" since truly human work is begun when each of these three aspects "exists together in a mutual interdependent relationship."[3] The instrumental aspect of work refers to the understanding of work as a means to a certain end, such as personal sustenance, economic growth, or spiritual purposes.[4] The relational aspect refers to "work's aims toward appropriate social relationships and/or to some form of human existential realization and fulfillment."[5] The ontological aspect refers to the intrinsic value of work. Work has been "built into the fabric of creation by God." Human beings are workers, "not as an accident of nature but because God first is a worker and persons are created in His image."[6] At the heart of various attempts to develop a theology of work is an attempt to find the intrinsic meaning and purpose of work beyond what is more commonly understood as merely instrumental, with the hope that these attempts would serve Christians in their struggle to integrate, or at least to connect, their faith and their work life.

The Present Theologies of Work

Paul Stevens,[7] writing a theology of work from a biblical theology perspective, summarizes various theological approaches to develop a theology of work so far: (a) Trinitarian theologies, in which human work is determined by the work of the Triune God;[8] (b) Creation theologies, in which human

---

2. Cosden, 4–5.
3. Cosden, 10.
4. Cosden, 11.
5. Cosden, 12.
6. Cosden, 17.
7. Stevens, *Work Matters*.
8. E.g. Schumacer, *God at Work*; Banks, *God the Worker*; Jensen, *Responsive Labor*.

work is viewed as a part of God's design in the creation of human beings;[9] (c) Image of God theologies, in which humans as God's image are given power to make decisions that makes a difference in this world;[10] (d) Curse theologies, in which work is understood to come after the Fall;[11] (e) New Creation theologies, in which work is perceived as an expression of life under the New Covenant, therefore is both redeemed and redeeming;[12] (f) Vocation theologies, in which work is perceived as a calling from God;[13] Spirit theologies, in which work is understood as an expression of the Spirit's work and gifts in the world;[14] (g) Kingdom theologies, in which the present work is perceived as part of an expression of God's life-giving and shalom-bringing rule in his kingdom;[15] and (h) Heaven and End Times theologies, in which the meaning of work is determined by Christian eschatological hope.[16]

A series of books on the theology of work from various church tradition perspectives were also published recently from: (a) Reformed perspective;[17] (b) Pentecostal perspective;[18] (c) Baptist perspective;[19] and (d) Wesleyan perspective.[20] While articles on the theology of work from the Roman Catholic perspective were also published,[21] a growing number of dissertations on the theme of faith and work integration or theology of work could also be identified, particularly in the past ten years.[22]

---

9. E.g. Haughey, *Converting Nine to Five*; Sherman and Hendricks, *Your Work Matters*; Ryken, *Work and Leisure*.

10. E.g. Bakke, *Joy at Work*; Larive, *After Sunday*.

11. E.g. Terkel, *Working*; Rifkin, *End of Work*.

12. E.g. Wyszynski, *All You Who Labor*.

13. E.g. Schuurman, *Vocation*; Hardy, *Fabric*.

14. E.g. Volf, *Work in the Spirit*; Marshall, *God @ Work*.

15. E.g. Witherington III, *Work*.

16. E.g. Cosden, *Theology of Work, Heavenly Good*; Marshall and Gilbert, *Heaven Is Not My Home*.

17. Bolt, *Economic Shalom*.

18. Self, *Flourishing Churches and Communities*.

19. Brand, *Flourishing Faith*.

20. Wright, *How God Makes the World a Better Place*.

21. E.g. Perricone, "Catholic Theology of Work and Worship"; Hamant, *Pioneer in Roman Catholic Social Thought*.

22. E.g. Burkey, "Theology of Work"; Browne, "On Faith and Work"; Fletcher, "Restoring the Sense of Divine Vocation to Work"; Jolley, "Bridging the Gap."

Together with 1,200 marketplace faith-related books, most written in the past three decades, listed by Pete Hammond in *The Marketplace Annotated Bibliography*, all these writings express a growing concern to integrate faith and work from a biblical perspective in contemporary Christianity.

Most of these diverse approaches are rooted or related to the most common feature of vocation as the classic model of theology of work among the Protestant, and protology, the doctrines surrounding the initial creation. Significant departures from this traditional approach that have significant influence in today's theology of work are the pneumatological instead of vocational approach and the eschatological instead of protological approach. Therefore, to provide an overview of literature on the theology of work, each of these basic approaches will be presented, together with the pros and cons around them.

Work as Vocation

Protestant understandings of work have been largely shaped by the theme of vocation (Lt. *vocare*), identical to calling. Placher observes that in the early church (100–500 CE), calling (*Gr. klesis*) usually meant the call to become Christian. This was because becoming Christian was full of risk, including readiness to a break from family and society.[23] However, there was a shift of meaning in the medieval church (500–1500 CE). At the time when people were commonly born into Christian families and grew in Christian societies, "having a vocation" meant almost exclusively joining the priesthood or some monastic order. Ordinary work was considered to have little significance for spiritual life.[24]

Against this church-world dichotomy prevalent in his day, Luther attempted to eradicate this dualism by identifying mundane work as God's calling. In Luther's German translation of the Bible, Luther translated the Greek word for calling, *klesis* (1 Cor 7:20) as *beruf*, the ordinary German word for an occupation.[25] In his theological framework, Luther made a distinction between the kingdom of heaven and the kingdom of earth. The former locates our relationship with God, based upon faith; the latter locates

---

23. Placher, *Callings*, 6, 23.
24. Placher, 6, 108.
25. Placher, 7.

our relationships with our neighbors based upon love. Vocation refers to the specific call to love our neighbor through the duties attached to our social place or "station" within the earthly kingdom.[26] This station includes all types of human relationships, whether domestic (as husbands, wives, parents, or children) or social (as magistrates, masters, servants, farmers, or bakers). These callings are the concrete and specific ways of serving our neighbors. According to Luther, they are divine vocations, instituted by God himself to meet the needs of humanity. Thus, by working we participate in God's ongoing provision for humanity.[27]

While Calvin did not elaborate extensively on this theme, his solidarity with Luther on the religious value of work is obvious in his commentary on some biblical passages such as Luke 10:38–42. In contrast to the traditional allegorical interpretation that puts the preference of contemplative life above working life, Calvin argues that Martha's problem was not that she worked, but that she worked excessively.[28] For Calvin, all kinds of work, even work which seems to be lowly, provided it contributes to the common good, is precious in God's sight. This understanding was elaborated further by his followers into an understanding of the divinely intended order of human society. "On the Reformed understanding then, human life is to be lived out in a society of mutual service and support, each member contributing according to his specific talents and receiving according to his need."[29] Both Luther and Calvin insisted that all legitimate social roles are God's calling. Subsequently, the vocational framework becomes "a distinctive and influential feature of the Lutheran and Reformed wings of the Protestant Reformation."[30]

Vocation and Charisma

A significant departure from the dominant traditional approach of vocational framework was taken by Miroslav Volf. In response to the increasingly changing context of the world of work from a static agricultural world to

---

26. Hardy, *Fabric*, 46.
27. Hardy, 47.
28. Hardy, 54–56.
29. Hardy, 60.
30. Schuurman, *Vocation*, 4.

a dynamic industrial and information world, Volf argues that the dynamic modern societies need a dynamic understanding of work. "A single, permanent, salaried, and full-time form of employment has given way to multiple and frequently changing jobs," and hence, to him "the dead hand of 'vocation' needed to be lifted from the Christian idea of work" and to be replaced with more suitable perspective.[31]

Volf also criticizes the framework of vocation as "indifferent toward alienation of work," potentially creating "a dangerous ambiguity" between vocation and occupation, and "easily misused ideologically." He argues that

> Since the notion of vocation suggests that every employment is
> a place of service to God – even when human activity in work is
> reduced to "soulless movement" – this notion functions simply
> to ennoble dehumanizing work in a situation where the quality
> of work should be improved through structural or other kinds
> of change. The vocational understanding of work provides no
> resources to foster such change.[32]

The alternative framework that Volf suggests is a pneumatological perspective of work developed within the eschatological framework. He argues that compared to the vocational perspective, the pneumatological perspective has a stronger relationship between the spiritual and external calling, is less open to ideological misuse of dehumanizing work, compared to vocation, and is easily conformed to the increasing diachronic and synchronic plurality in the industrial and information societies. Furthermore,

> In the vocational understanding of work, God addresses hu-
> man beings, calling them to work, and they respond to God's
> call primarily by obedience. They work out a sense of duty. In
> a pneumatological understanding of work, God does not first
> and foremost command human beings to work, but empowers
> and gifts them for work. They work, not primarily because it is
> their duty to work, but because they experience the inspiration

---

31. Volf, *Work in the Spirit*, vii.
32. Volf, 108.

and enabling of God's Spirit and can do the will of God "from the heart." (Eph 6:6: cf. Col 3:23)[33]

A year before Volf published his *Work in the Spirit*, Hardy's book *The Fabric of This World* discussed how Reformed tradition addressed the problem in Luther's notion of "station" without leaving the vocational framework. "Whereas for Luther our vocation is discerned in the duties of our station life, for the Calvinists it is derived from our gifts. We have a duty to use our talents and abilities for our neighbor's sake . . . The station is no longer normative, but must be judged by its suitability as an instrument of social service."[34]

In response to Volf, Hardy, acknowledging that there is much to be commended in Volf's theology of work, questions the need to replace the "old" vocational understanding with the "new" charismatic paradigm.[35] Hardy highlights the fact that the language of gifts in the Protestant theology of work has been used since the time of Reformation. "One can find it already in Calvin; and it comes to full expression in the practical theology of the Puritans, who regularly spoke of vocation in terms of gifts and mutual service – both in the church and in the world."[36] To Hardy's point, as early as the beginning of the seventeenth century, William Perkins, one of the leading Puritan theologians, in *A Treatise of the Vocations* has linked the notion of gifts instead of "station" to calling: "everyone, rich or poor, man or woman, is bound to have a personal calling in which they must perform some duties for the common good, according to the measure of the gifts that God has bestowed upon them."[37]

Until recently, many authors held the vocational framework as a bigger umbrella in approaching work. Important as it is, talents or gifts are considered to be only one among other factors to people's understanding of calling. As Frederick Buechner says, "the place God calls you into is the place where your deep gladness and the world's deep hunger meet."[38] Vocation,

---

33. Volf, 125.
34. Hardy, *Fabric*, 66.
35. Hardy, "Review."
36. Hardy, 195.
37. Perkins, *Treatise of the Vocations*, 267.
38. Buechner, *Wishful Thinking*, 119.

as promoted by Luther and echoed by various authors until recently, also connects work life with other dimensions of life, including family life and social life. Vocation is not limited to paid occupation. Each role, as a parent, a child, a parishioner, a citizen or other entails a specific vocation.[39] Thus, work can be seen in a larger context.

Protology and Eschatology

Most approaches in developing a theology of work are protological, in which the creation account becomes the starting point to develop theological reflections on work. The protological approach is rich in resources to provide the foundational pattern in developing a theology of work. The creation account, especially the account in which human beings are made in the image of God and the cultural mandate in Genesis 1:27–28 have become the basis for developing the intrinsic value of work,[40] while the account of the fall has become the basis for understanding the roots of the present problems of work.[41]

However, protology alone has proved to leave a gap that was unintentionally filled by an instrumental understanding of work. As in Luther's case, comprehending work merely from the protological perspective may affirm the purpose and meaning of work as an act of service to God and others in the present life, but the comprehension still leaves room to misunderstand ordinary work as merely a part of this earthly kingdom and to find its eternal value only in service to the heavenly kingdom. The hierarchy of work value based on its spiritual impact then becomes unavoidable. Certain types of spiritual work such as that done by pastors and missionaries are seen to be more meaningful than secular types of work such as that done by lawyers and businesspeople. This hierarchical understanding of work is still quite pervasive even until recently.[42]

A radical shift to the eschatological approach was developed by Volf and elaborated further by Cosden drawing from the eschatological vision of

---

39. Hardy, *Fabric*, 82.

40. E.g. Sherman and Hendricks, *Your Work Matters*; Ryken, *Work and Leisure*; Bakke, *Joy at Work*; Larive, *After Sunday*.

41. E.g. Terkel, *Working*; and Rifkin, *End of Work*.

42. Cosden, *Heavenly Good*, 43–47; Sherman, *Kingdom Calling*, 64–76.

Jurgen Moltmann.[43] Volf argues that a proper understanding of eschatology is crucial to establish the foundation of a theology of work. He differentiates eschatological views: *annihilatio mundi*, the "radical" discontinuity between the present and future orders because of the annihilation of the old creation, including human work, and *transformatio mundi*, the continuity of the old creation that will be transformed into the new creation. He insists that without such continuity human work is "devoid of direct ultimate significance,"[44] since "It is hard to believe in the intrinsic value and goodness of something that God will completely annihilate."[45] He argues rather that the results of human work "after being purified in the eschatological *transformatio mundi*, will be integrated by an act of divine transformation into the new heaven and the new earth."[46]

Sharing a similar view with Volf, Cosden argues "our ordinary work affects and in some ways actually adds to (though it does not cause, determine or bring about) the ultimate shape of eternity – the new creation. When we grasp this eternal aspect of work, we will have begun to experience the fullness of God's intended purpose for us and for our work."[47] The reason behind this claim is that the pervasive sense of meaninglessness toward secular work at present is rooted in the strong influence of dualism in the western society. Cosden criticizes Luther because in his division of Christian life between the spiritual or heavenly kingdom and the earthly kingdom, he has created a misunderstanding that ordinary work does not have eternal value.[48] This line of thinking reaffirms dualism and hierarchy of callings in the protestant church, between work that is perceived to have eternal impact and temporary impact.

Modern Roman Catholic teaching on work can be traced back to Pope Leo XIII's encyclical *Rerum Novarum* (the worker's charter) in 1891. *Rerum Novarum* is a sign of a radical shift in Roman Catholic perspective on work from their instrumental perspective that lasted for centuries since the middle

43. Volf, *Work in the Spirit*; Cosden, *Theology of Work, Heavenly Good*.

44. Volf, *Work in the Spirit*, 89.

45. Volf, 91.

46. Volf, 92.

47. Cosden, *Heavenly Good*, 2.

48. Cosden, 43–47.

ages.[49] A fuller development of the official Roman Catholic view on work can be found almost one century later in Pope John Paul II's encyclical *Laborem Exercens* (*On Human Work*) in 1981. Cosden highlights its uniqueness in its focusing on human work in contrast to other encyclicals which usually cover a range of social issues.[50] Human work is stated as the "key, probably the essential key, to the whole social question" (Laborem Exercens, part 3). This document addresses the instrumental, relational, and ontological aspects of work. However, Cosden also criticizes *Laborem Exercens* because it reaffirms spirit-matter dualism in its division between the "objective sense of work" (i.e. work's material nature and product) and the "subjective sense of work" (i.e. the impact of work on us as persons existentially, socially, and spiritually).[51] Based on this division, the hierarchical ordering of the latter over the former is emphasized based on the conviction of "the superiority of spirit over matter."

Cosden insists that, even though radical shifts have happened in both Protestant and Catholic churches, "in most basic form, a spirit-material dualism (or hierarchy) has in fact been a building block in western thinking for most of the last two millennia – and in western theology, both Catholic and Protestant . . . "[52] Therefore, for Cosden, following Volf, the cure lies in the eschatological approach in understanding work.

Addressing the interpretation of the fire of judgment in 2 Peter 3:7 that is often used by those who argue for discontinuity, Cosden argues that it refers to the fire of purification of this earth and everything in it rather than destroying to replace it.[53] God's judgment will destroy all traces of sin and death in human being as well as human culture. However, the best results of our works will be transformed and incorporated into the new creation. Moreover, rather than thinking of them as individual products, they are to be viewed as part of the "fabric of this world," namely the best development

---

49. Cosden, *Theology of Work*, 20.
50. Cosden, 25.
51. Cosden, *Heavenly Good*, 27.
52. Cosden, 24.
53. Cosden, 113.

found in human culture that will be transformed into the "fabric of the new earth."[54]

Langer critiques both Volf's and Cosden's view arguing that from a biblical perspective the relationship between the old and new creation can be described by both metaphors of transformation and annihilation. Langer maintains that eschatological transformation is discontinuous and continuous at the same time so that "single metaphors are simply inadequate for describing the eschatological transformation between old and new creations."[55] This transformation, he insists is evident in the different metaphors used by Paul to describe the relationship between our current body and our resurrection body that refer to both discontinuity (e.g. the destruction of our body in 2 Cor 5:1) and continuity (e.g. the metaphors of waking and sleeping in 1 Cor 15: 20, 52, 53).

Furthermore, Langer says putting too much emphasis on the participation of the result of our work in the new heaven and the new earth might not be helpful for us to understand the significance of our work, particularly when we are told that our contribution is only a tiny part to the huge building of the overall development of human culture. Langer also warns of the danger of falling into utopic dreams of the future through our works in this fallen world, especially if we embrace the first view that overstresses the continuity of the result of our work. Thus, he suggests understanding work as anticipatory rather than participatory. "It can pass away, having fulfilled its purpose if it creates an authentic anticipation of Christ's kingdom in the present world – at least for a moment – glimmer with the light of the next."[56]

Another question related to our work in the new creation is will we still work in the new heaven and the new earth? Davis argues convincingly that there will be work in the new creation. "If God continues to work in acts of creation and providence, redeemed humans in the new creation will continue to reflect the Creator by caring for fellow creatures and by engaging in new, creative acts of arts, invention, culture, and worship."[57] A similar view is also taken by others. Stevens, for example, emphasizes that since work is part of

---

54. Cosden, 115.
55. Langer, "Niggle's Leaf," 105.
56. Langer, 113.
57. Davis, "Will There Be New Work," 260.

our human nature, expecting people not to work in the new creation would mean "we would stop being human!"[58] As has been highlighted by Volf and Cosden on the glorified work in the New Jerusalem, the eschatological vision of the city life indicates the need for its inhabitant to work for mutual service and also the appreciation of the development of human culture in the present world.[59] In fact, Cosden describes this point very well in his first book, *A Theology of Work: Work and the New Creation,* when he elaborates his second thesis in that book on the ontological dimension of work. However, in his attempt to oppose the misguiding dualistic notion of work (spirit over matter), in Cosden's second book, *The Heavenly Good of Earthly Work,* there is a shift of emphasis from the lasting nature of work to a more problematic emphasis on the lasting fruits of work. As it has been discussed earlier, the claim for the latter is proven to be exegetically inconclusive.

The Whole Biblical Story as the Framework

Away from the debate of whether the vocational and protological framework should be replaced either by pneumatological and eschatological approach are those who embrace both the old and new approaches selectively. While they retain the vocational framework, they also modify it in accordance with the more dynamic modern workplace situation. Instead of a static calling in certain occupation for the whole life (as originally proposed by Luther), gifts, talents, and abilities are to be used as indications to find the best way to serve neighbors as a response to God's calling.[60] While starting their theological reflection from creation, they also recognize the significance of the eschatological vision to establish a more complete biblical perspective on work.[61]

Some authors promote the fourfold framework of the biblical story or biblical meta narrative as the framework to understand the meaning and purpose of human work. John Stott argues that the Bible divides human history into epochs marked by four major events: the creation ("the good"), the fall ("the evil"), the redemption ("the new"), and the consummation ("the perfect"). He maintains that the four events "especially when grasped

---

58. Stevens, *Work Matters,* 163.

59. Volf, *Work in the Spirit*; Cosden, *Theology of Work.*

60. E.g. Hardy, *Fabric*; Sherman, *Kingdom Calling.*

61. E.g. Stevens, *Doing God's Business*; *Work Matters*; Sherman, *Kingdom Calling*; Keller and Alsdorf, *Every Good Endeavor.*

in relation to one another, teach major truths about God, human beings and society which give direction to our Christian thinking."[62]

Christopher Wright, based on this fourfold scheme of biblical history, develops a comprehensive picture of God's mission in the biblical story and its connection with how God's people could participate in that mission through their daily work.[63] Other examples of how this framework is used are by Van Duzer as the structure for his book, *Why Business Matters: And What Still Needs to be Fixed,* by Amy Sherman in her *Kingdom Calling: Vocational Stewardship for the Common Good,* and briefly referred to as the Christian worldview to understand work in Tim Keller and Katherine Alsdorf's *Every Good Endeavor: Connecting Your Work to God's Work.*

Albert Wolters in his *Creation Regained: Biblical Basis for a Reformational Worldview,* although he used only creation, fall, and redemption as a skeleton for his writing, also describe the fourth pillar of consummation in his classic formulation of integrated Christian worldview, in which the meaning and purpose of work are very well explained. Wolters argues that the "creation mandate" or the "cultural mandate" in Genesis 1:28 is foundational. The six days of creation account in Genesis 1 describes how God formed and filled the originally unformed and empty earth. Human beings, as God's image, are given the mandate to continue the work. "People must now carry on the work of development: by being fruitful they must fill it even more; by subduing it they must form it even more."[64] Through cultural mandate, human beings "are called to participate in the ongoing creational work of God, to be God's helper in executing to the end the blueprint for his masterpiece."[65]

Wolters also stresses that "the ravages of sin do not annihilate the normative creational development of civilization, but rather are parasitical upon it."[66] Likening the world to an originally healthy newborn baby who contracts a serious chronic disease that caused her to become an invalid, Christ's redemptive work is pictured as a cure so that while it "counteracts and nullifies the action of the disease," the purpose is to enable the normal

---

62. Stott, *Issues Facing Christians Today,* 64.
63. Wright, *Mission of God's People.*
64. Wolters, *Creation Regained,* 41.
65. Wolters, 42.
66. Wolters, 46.

development of the body.[67] In Cosden's words, salvation has a twofold meaning: restoring us "to the place where we fell from (our initial purpose)" and
also taking us "beyond our beginning to where God always intended to
bring us (to fulfill that purpose)."[68]

In combining both the continuity and discontinuity of human culture
into the new heaven and earth, Wolters sums up the eschatological perspective of human work:

> There is no reason to doubt that they will be transfigured and
> transformed by their liberation from the curse, but they will be
> in essential continuity with our experience now – just as our
> resurrected bodies, though glorified, will still be bodies. It may
> be as Herman Bavinck has suggested, that human life on the
> new earth, compared to that life now, will be like the colorful
> butterfly that develops out of the pupa: dramatically different,
> but the same creature.[69]

Work and Mission

Development of the Theology of Mission

In Bosch's classic work *Transforming Mission*, he asserts that until the 1950s
"mission" had been understood in a set of circumscribed meanings: "(a) the
sending of missionaries to a designated territory, (b) the activities undertaken
by such missionaries, (c) the geographical area where the missionaries were
active, (d) the agency which dispatched the missionaries, (e) the non-Christian world or 'mission-field,' or (f) the center from which the missionaries
operated on the 'mission field.'"[70] Together with the remarkable escalation
in the use of the word "mission" among Christians in the second half of
the twentieth century, there has been a broadening, if not the shift of the

---

67. Wolters, 46.
68. Cosden, *Heavenly Good*, 79.
69. Wolters, *Creation Regained*, 48.
70. Bosch, *Transforming Mission*, 1.

concept. This is related to the major changes in the world that have caused a paradigm shift in missiology.[71]

Following Tomas Kuhn's paradigm theory that was used by Hans Kung to divide Christianity into six eras, in accordance with six major paradigms that influenced the way Christians in those eras understand their faith peculiarly, Bosch argues that Christians have also understood mission differently in those six historical epochs which are (1) primitive Christianity, (2) the patristic period, (3) the middle ages, (4) the Reformation, (5) the Enlightenment, and (6) the ecumenical era.[72] As reality changed significantly, people in the following era "perceive reality in ways qualitatively different from their predecessors" and hence a new "paradigm" (theoretical structure) is developed.

From another point of view, Craig Ott, tracing back to the historical development since the earliest Protestant mission efforts, observes that there are four major ways in which the task of mission is understood and practiced by the church from the reformation to the present.[73] They are: (1) proclamation and conversion, (2) church planting and growth, (3) civilization and moral improvement, and (4) philanthropy, humanization, and liberation. While in practice these lines are not mutually exclusive, during the twentieth century the first three were more commonly emphasized in evangelical circles, and the last one was more common in ecumenical circles. This reflects the split between evangelism and social concern, or between proclamation and action in mission, particularly in the first half of the twentieth century.

Up to the nineteenth century, division between evangelism and social action in Christian missions was not a common phenomenon. William Carey, for example, "the father of modern missions" is well-known for his all-round efforts in both evangelism and social reform in India.[74] However, a "Great Reversal" was going on in the beginning of the twentieth century, and evangelicals retreated almost totally from the mainstream society.[75] Tizon identifies at least two explanations for this. First, there was a counter-reaction to the increasing influence of liberal theology that emphasized social concern

---

71. Bosch, 1.
72. Bosch, 187–188.
73. Ott and Strauss, *Encountering Theology*, 106–136.
74. Tizon, "Precursors and Tensions," 62.
75. cf. Moberg, *Great Reversal*.

at the expense of evangelism. Second, there was a shift from a predominantly post-millennial to pre-millennial eschatology that erased any hope for a better world before Christ's second coming. "By the late 1920s, to be evangelical meant, for most, identification with pre-millennial fundamentalism that reactively erased social responsibility from the missionary agenda."[76]

The evangelism-social concern debate in protestant missions was going on in the midst of the larger debate over the ultimate meaning of mission between evangelicals and ecumenicals. Ignited by the 1932 publication of William Hocking's *Re-Thinking Missions* that denied the uniqueness of Christianity and declared the purpose of mission was to seek religious cooperation with other faiths toward a better world, the polarization between the evangelicals and the ecumenical was widened in the following decades.[77]

Toward the end of the twentieth century, however, there has been moderation in both positions and reconciliation between evangelical and conciliar missiologists. While in the ecumenical circle the pendulum is swinging toward the recognition of the role of the church and the place for evangelism in its mission,[78] in the evangelical circle the pendulum is swinging toward to a more holistic perspective of mission that includes social concern together with evangelism.[79]

Holistic Mission

Las Newman in the "Foreword" of *Holistic Mission: God's Plan for God's People* states, "One of the most important developments in contemporary Christian missiology is the recovery of a theology of mission in the late twentieth century that integrates faith and life, word and deed, proclamation and presence."[80] This understanding is not a new invention, "but deeply further in the biblical theology of Judeo-Christian faith of the Old and New Testaments."[81]

A significant turning point toward a more holistic perspective on mission in the evangelical circle took place at the Lausanne Conference in 1974

---

76. Tizon, "Precursors and Tensions," 62.

77. Tizon, 63.

78. Bosch, *Transforming Mission*, 389, 409.

79. Ott and Strauss, *Encountering Theology*, 137.

80. Woolnough and Ma, *Holistic Mission*, ix.

81. Woolnough and Ma, ix.

that brought together 2,300 evangelical leaders from 150 countries. It was affirmed in this conference that "evangelism and sociopolitical involvement are both part of our Christian duty," and hence social concern was to be included in mission.[82] In the Lausanne Covenant section 6, "Mission and Evangelism," it was also asserted that "World evangelization requires the whole Church to take the whole gospel to the whole world."[83]

In 1975 John Stott, the leading thinker in the Lausanne Movement, published *Christian Mission in the Modern World*, claiming the primacy of the Great Commission in John 17:18 and 20:21 (to be sent as Jesus was sent) over Matthew 28:16–20 (to make disciples). According to Stott, social action is an equal partner with evangelism, even though he kept the primacy of evangelism in mission.[84] By the 1980s numerous publications and consultations were launched to discuss further the evangelical perspective on the place of social action and its relationship with evangelism in mission.[85] In the "Consultation on the Church in Response to Human Need" in 1983, which was sponsored by the World Evangelical Fellowship, the discussion shifted further from social responsibility to holistic mission. Significant amounts of literature advocating holistic mission and social action from various evangelical thinkers were also published during these years to develop a solid biblical ground for this position.[86] Some argue for Jesus as the model for ministering to the whole person. Others emphasized the kingdom of God as a framework to understand the comprehensive nature of mission beyond merely evangelism or social action.[87]

The shift back to a more holistic understanding of mission was not without reservation. McGavran, for example, insists on the primacy of evangelism and church planting in mission.[88] To him those would lead to personal and social change. Hesselgrave, another ardent critic of holistic mission,

---

82. Woolnough and Ma, 4–5.

83. Lausanne Movement, "The Lausanne Covenant."

84. Ott and Strauss, *Encountering Theology*, 139.

85. Ott and Strauss, 140.

86. E.g. Costas, *Church and Its Mission, Integrity of Mission, Christ Outside the Gate*; Escobar and Diver, *Christian Mission*; Dyrness, *Let the Earth Rejoice*; Padilla, *Mission Between the Times*.

87. Ott and Strauss, *Encountering Theology*, 141.

88. McGavran, *Understanding Church Growth*.

maintains that Matthean formulation of the Great Commission is the final and most complete statement on mission, not John 20:21.[89] Hesselgrave promotes what he calls the traditional view of "prioritism" (in contrast to holism) which does not rule out social action in missions but asserts evangelism and church planting are a priority.[90]

Ott notes two reasons that complicate further the debates and tension within the evangelical movement. Much of the polarization emerged from the difference between the historical and contextual background, between those who fear that evangelical mission will neglect evangelism and those who are impatient with the status quo mentality in facing pressing social problems of poverty and injustice. The differences are not so far apart in practice, and both groups, in fact, do evangelism and social action in their mission work.

While the tension still remains, acceptance of a holistic understanding of mission keeps growing, and currently it is widely accepted among the evangelicals.[91] Wright, in the remarks of *Holistic Mission: God's Plan for God's People*,[92] notes that Lausanne 2010 in Cape Town, the world mission conference of the evangelical movement, marks the consolidation of a return to an integrated and holistic understanding of mission. Further commitment to integral mission was asserted, and a third major issue of creation care was also included:

> Integral mission means discerning, proclaiming, and living out, the biblical truth that the gospel is God's good news, through the cross and resurrection of Jesus Christ, for individual persons, and for society, and for creation. All three are broken and suffering because of sin: all three are included in the redeeming love and mission of God: all three must be part of the comprehensive mission of God's people.[93]

---

89. Hesselgrave, "Redefining Holism."

90. Hesselgrave, *Paradigms in Conflict*; Ott and Strauss, *Encountering Theology*, 142–143.

91. Tizon, "Precursors and Tensions"; cf. Padilla, "Holistic Mission."

92. Woolnough and Ma, *Holistic Mission*.

93. Lausanne Movement, "Cape Town Commitment."

Similar understanding of a comprehensive nature of mission among the ecumenical movement is also reflected in Bosch's description of the emerging ecumenical missionary paradigm in the twentieth century. At the end of his thorough analysis, he concludes and proposes that mission is a multifaceted ministry:

> Mission is a multifaceted ministry, in respect of witness, service, justice, healing, reconciliation, liberation, peace, evangelism, fellowship, church planting, contextualization, and much more. And yet, even the attempt to list some dimensions of mission is fraught with danger, because it again suggests that we can define what is infinite. Whoever we are, we are tempted to incarcerate the *missio Dei* in the narrow confines of our predilections, thereby of necessity reverting to one-sidedness and reductionism.[94]

Without necessarily simplifying the diversity of multiple perspectives within this global movement, a similar perspective of mission is also indicated in the "WCC 2013 Resource Book" for the most recent World Council of Churches (WCC) conference in 2013 in Busan, South Korea.

Mission as *Missio Dei*

At the very foundation of the holistic understanding of mission is that "mission" is the mission of God. In fact, until the sixteenth century the term "mission" was used exclusively to refer to the Trinity, namely the sending of the Son by the Father and of the Holy Spirit by the Father and the Son. It was the Jesuits who first used the word "mission" to describe their activities in spreading their Christian faith to those who were not members of the Catholic church.[95] Bosch notes that in the second half of the twentieth century there has been a subtle but decisive shift toward the recovery of understanding of mission as *missio Dei*.[96] Karl Barth was one of the first theologians known to articulate that mission is an activity of God himself. The *missio Dei* concept was affirmed in the International Mission Conference

---

94. Bosch, *Transforming Mission*, 512.
95. Bosch, 1.
96. Bosch, 389–393.

1952 at Willingen. Bosch notes that afterwards the understanding of *missio Dei* "has been embraced by virtually all Christian persuasions" – first by conciliar or ecumenical Protestants but subsequently by other ecclesial groupings, such as the Eastern Orthodox, evangelicals, and also endorsed in Catholic mission theology in the Second Vatican Council.[97]

The concept of *missio Dei* refers to the understanding that mission is primarily God's activity. "God is reaching out to His world through Christ and His Spirit. He is engaged in liberating the cosmos and humankind from captivity of evil, and it is His purpose to gather the whole creation under the Lordship of Christ."[98] This means, "All our missions flow from the prior mission of God."[99] He has a mission, a purpose and goal for his whole creation. His mission is what Paul called as the "whole will of God" (Acts 20:27; cf. Eph 1:9–10). And he called us to participate in the fulfillment of that divine mission. Therefore, the scope is much wider than what can be found in the Great Commission at the end of the Gospel of Matthew. "God's mission is what spans the gap between the curse and the end of the curse in the new creation of Revelation 22 . . . It is a vast, comprehensive project of cosmic salvation."[100]

In accordance with this understanding, Wright, in *The Mission of God's People* develops a thorough biblical theology of mission. In it he develops a comprehensive picture of God's mission in the biblical story, and how the whole of God's people could participate in that mission. This holistic picture of mission could be summarized using three sets of key phrases from "The Lausanne Covenant": the whole gospel, the whole world, and the whole church.

The Whole Gospel

Wright asserts that the glorious richness of the gospel of God is that it can transform every area of human life contaminated by sin. He argues for the cosmic scope of the gospel as stated in Colossians 1:15–20 so that "The cross must be central to every dimension of the mission of God's people – from

---

97. Bosch, 390–391.
98. Peskett and Ramachandra, *Message of Mission*, 29.
99. Wright, *Mission of God's People*, 24.
100. Wright, 46.

personal evangelism among individual friends to ecological care for creation, and everything in between."[101]

The Whole World

A holistic mission based on the whole gospel would include the whole aspect of humanity as the target of restoration: physical, intellectual, emotional, and social. It would also encompass the whole aspect of human relationships: with God, self, others, and the rest of creation. Furthermore, it would not limit the transforming power of the gospel merely to individuals, but it would extend mission to cultural and structural aspects of human societies as well.[102]

The Whole Church

Since the mission of God's people is to bring the transforming power of the gospel into every area of human life, and even to the whole creation, it would involve the whole church at the frontline. The whole gospel based on the whole biblical story does not recognize a division between sacred and secular works. The callings of pastors, evangelists, and missionaries are not higher than businessmen, engineers, farmers, and those who have other "secular" jobs. They just have different roles to play in a huge orchestra of the mission of God's people to bring the whole gospel to the whole world.[103]

While theology of work has provided a robust framework to understand the intrinsic meaning of work and to affirm human beings as God's image with a cultural mandate, Wright's thorough exposition on biblical mission provides a robust theological framework to understand the connection between daily human works with God's mission. Therefore, Steve Garber's statement is an accurate summary of this holistic framework. "Vocation is integral, not incidental, to *missio Dei.*"[104]

Work and Cultural Engagement

But how do we relate to our non-Christian friends who at times seem to be more capable of contributing to society through their cultivation and

---

101. Wright, 43.
102. Wright, 43.
103. Wright, 272.
104. Garber, *Visions of Vocation*, 137.

creativity? The four pillars of the biblical meta-narrative (creation, fall, re-demption, consummation) will help us to understand this situation. From the creation perspective, because all human beings are made in the image of God and are bestowed with cultural gifts to fulfill their cultural mandate, "we should not be surprised that many people without belief in Jesus can do great work – even better work – than Christians."[105] Similarly, Hunter reminds us of the reality of the universality of the "common grace" that enables "people of every creed and no creed have talents and abilities, possess knowledge, wisdom, and inventiveness, and hold standards of goodness, truth, justice, morality, and beauty that are, in relative degree, in harmony with God's will and purposes."[106] This does not necessarily mean that Christians do not have a unique role in their calling. From the redemption perspective, Christians are those who have been redeemed and called to proclaim and embody Christ's redemptive power in their lives, including to bring "the foretastes" of God's eschatological shalom through their daily work.[107]

This tension suggests a humble attitude for Christians in fulfilling their calling, as God's agents of transformation and participants of his work, not as the author of the transformation.[108] Hunter suggests that Christians embrace this humble attitude of "faithful presence" in fulfilling their calling to bring the foretastes of shalom in all areas of life.[109] First, it means "that we are to be fully present to each other within the community of faith and fully present to those who are not . . . and direct our lives toward the flourishing of each other through sacrificial love."[110] Second, it "requires that Christians be fully present and committed to their tasks . . . What we do certainly would include our jobs, but the reality is that our tasks are many, and they range far beyond paid labor. They involve our work as parents, students, volunteers, citizens, and the like." Third, it means "that Christians are fully present and

---

105. Keller and Alsdorf, *Every Good Endeavor*, 185.

106. Hunter, *To Change the World*, 232.

107. Sherman, *Kingdom Calling*.

108. Crouch, *Culture Making*.

109. Hunter, *To Change the World*.

110. Hunter, 244.

committed in their spheres of social influence, whatever they may be: their families, neighborhoods, voluntary activities, and places of work."[111]

Marketplace Mission Movements

The growing awareness of the need to pursue the integration of faith, work, and mission was to a significant extent reflected in the emergence of three new issue groups in the 2004 Lausanne conference in Thailand: marketplace ministry, business as mission, and tentmaking. Johnson and Rundle claim that these movements, together with Enterprise Development, are "four camps within a single movement."[112] This classification of the "contemporary marketplace mission movement"[113] is consistently used, with slightly changes in definitions, by the proponents of Business as Mission (BAM).[114]

Rundle in "Restoring the Role of Business in Mission" lists a summary of the distinction of each movement as: (1) Tentmaking: "often used to describe individual Christians who find employment in a cross-cultural context, taking jobs in schools, hospitals or business, etc;" (2) Marketplace Ministry: "used in reference to parachurch organizations that disciple and coach Christian business professionals to be more an effective witness in the workplace. Increasingly, the term 'Workplace Ministry' is being used instead which broadens the focus to include all working professionals;" (3) BAM refers to "businesses (often called 'Great Commission Companies' or 'Kingdom business') that are created and managed specifically for the purpose of advancing the cause of Christ in less-reached and/or less-developed parts of the world," and (4) Christian Microenterprise Development: "seeks to help the world's poorest people start and run successful, God-honoring business, often with the help of small loans."[115]

Liu, Preece, and Wong in the Lausanne Occasional Paper refer to Marketplace Ministry as "applying to all workplace areas by laying down certain theological foundations that others have built on and applied to

---

111. Hunter, 247.

112. Johnson and Rundle, "Business as Mission," 21–26.

113. Johnson, *Business as Mission*.

114. E.g. in Liu et al., "Lausanne Occasional Paper No. 40"; Johnson and Rundle, "Business as Mission;" Johnson, *Business as Mission*; Rundle, "Restoring."

115. Rundle, "Restoring," 760–761.

their more specialized area,"[116] which includes Tentmaking, BAM, and Student Diaspora. The different approach to the classification within what Johnson called the "Marketplace Mission Movement" indicated in his notes that the distinctions between and among the camps within the movement are far from clear.[117] Marketplace Ministry, in a wider sense of definition includes working professionals, not merely business leaders and entrepreneurs.[118] Johnson further subdivides this movement as: (a) general marketplace ministries; (b) association of marketplace ministries; (c) for-profit marketplace ministry entrepreneurs; (d) Christian professional associations, affinity groups and guilds; (e) church and parachurch-based marketplace ministries; (f) academic institutions and academicians focusing on faith and work integration; (g) marketplace ministry activists, and (h) organizations supporting marketplace ministries.[119] According to Johnson, motives behind this movement are various:

> To evangelize and disciple the lost within the marketplace; to provide mutual encouragement, mentoring and support for Christians within the marketplace; to equip marketplace leaders to lead their companies for Christ; to discern how to apply Scripture to the rough-and-tumble. Work-a-day world with its own particular business ethic and credo; to learn how to live out one's faith on a 24/7 basis; and to discover ways that they can balance work with home, family, recreation, and church.[120]

The development of the Marketplace Mission Movement looks promising. However, a closer scrutiny is needed to clarify whether BAM and the other "camps" in the Marketplace Mission Movement have developed a holistic approach to mission that promotes the intrinsic value of work that they claim [121]The tentmaking approach for example, often implies work as merely an instrument for the real mission, which is evangelism and church planting. Another example related to the marketplace ministry is recent

116. Liu, Preece, and Wong, "Marketplace Ministry," 9.
117. Johnson, *Business as Mission*.
118. Rundle, "Restoring," 760–761.
119. Johnson, *Business as Mission*.
120. Johnson, 131.
121. Johnson and Rundle, "Business as Mission."

research conducted in the American context which also indicates that most of the marketplace ministries being studied focused on evangelism and discipleship in the workplace, but they missed "deeper, richer, more creative faith/work integration."[122] Together with the previous examples, the statements regarding BAM itself that look at the business marketplace as the mission field or as a strategy of choice for mission may indicate the ongoing tension between prioritism and holism in the understanding of holistic mission. While a grasp of holism is closely related to the strong awareness of the intrinsic value of work, prioritism tends to reflect the instrumental perspective of work itself and the dualistic view of the spirit over matter.

Vocational Stewardship

In her book, *Kingdom Calling: Vocational Stewardship for the Common Good*, Amy Sherman, coined the term "vocational stewardship" to refer to faith and work integration from a missional perspective. Vocational stewardship is defined as "the intentional and strategic deployment of our vocational power – knowledge, platform, networks, position, influence, skills and reputation – to advance foretastes of God's kingdom."[123] While Christian hope refers to the full restoration of this world under God's rule at the *eschaton* (end of time), it is believed to be a Christian duty to bring about the foretastes of grace, love, and justice among other values of the kingdom to come.

Using a metaphor of Christians as "the foretastes" of the coming kingdom, Sherman suggests Christians to be the *tsaddiqim* (the righteous) (Prov 11:10) in the present day. She suggests four pathways for Christians to fulfill this role through their work: (1) Bloom: promoting the kingdom in and through the person's daily work; (2) Donate: volunteering vocational talent outside the person's day job; (3) Invent: launching a new social enterprise; and (4) Invest: participating in the church's targeted initiative. She stresses that "bloom" is the "primary and most important avenue for deploying vocational power."[124]

Miller contends that various attempts of individuals and organizations to pursue faith and work integration could be divided into four types: ethic,

---

122. Sherman, *Kingdom Calling*, 95.
123. Sherman, 20.
124. Sherman, 144.

evangelism, experience, and enrichment. He suggests that those who have all the four types of integration as "Everywhere Integrators" are the most ideal. Commenting on Miller's analysis, Sherman claims that the Everywhere Integrator type of Miller is the closest to the concept of vocational steward-ship for the common good that she is promoting.[125] The *tsaddiqim* (the righteous) in her vocational stewardship take seriously all three dimensions of righteousness: vertical, internal, and social.

However, her own research indicated that it was not easy to find this ideal type in this current faith at work movement. The findings of her study of fifteen evangelical marketplace ministries, of which some of them bear the name "international" reflecting their ministry scope, show that most of them fall only into Miller's Ethics type or Evangelism type. Twelve of the fifteen groups were mainly focused on winning people to Christ through Bible studies, evangelism and prayer, and/or encouraging their members to be good witnesses in their workplace. Some of them showed elements of the Enrichment type, but none of them fit into the Experience type, in which the intrinsic value of work is recognized. None of the groups reflected the Everywhere Integrator type.

Another research conducted by Sherman and her team concerning twenty-three Christian professional societies also shows that "the majority of associations were more internally than externally focused."[126] About half of them had a significant focus on evangelism, not many had an explicit focus on ethics, and about a third focused on promoting excellence in their craft. Her findings suggest that only a few of these organizations fit Miller's category of the "Everywhere Integrator" type.

Based on her research and observations, Sherman laments that a vital part of the vocational stewardship for the common good that is missing in most of these groups is a vision for the transformation of the institutions where believers work. Vocational stewardship, she suggests, would include bringing the vision of *shalom* through a wide range of individual vocations, into every sphere of social life.[127]

---

125. Sherman, 95–96.
126. Sherman, 97.
127. Sherman, 99.

Formation for Vocational Stewardship

Spiritual Formation

Throughout centuries, spiritual formation has been understood in various ways across various Christian traditions.[128] Jeffrey Greenman observes that several key authors, notably Richard Foster, Dallas Willard, James Houston, and Eugene Peterson, have significantly shifted the focus of mainstream evangelical conversation from the traditional category of discipleship to a broader category of spiritual formation. He argues that the seminal work of Richard Foster in 1978, "The Celebration of Discipline," marked the birth of the evangelical spiritual formation movement.[129]

John Dettoni suggests five scriptural passages as a foundation to understand spiritual formation: Romans 12:2; Galatians 4:19; Matthew 28:19; Colossians 1:28–29; and Ephesians 4:13. Three key words he gleaned from these passages: formation, disciple, and maturity.

Formation. Spiritual formation (Gal 4:19) is closely related to the idea of transformation (Rom 12:2; 2 Cor 3:18). Formation and transformation have a similar root word *morphe* (Gk). The word transformation suggests "our central core being is transformed into something quite different. It is not just an outward change but a metamorphosis from one form to another new and better one."[130] This transformation includes knowledge, value system, and behavior.

Discipleship (Matt 28:19). It suggests "an active following of Jesus" by living "a life filled with prayer, quiet service, Scripture reading, meditation, worship, and fasting, to name a few," as spiritual disciplines behind Jesus's great acts.[131]

Maturity. The goal of transformation is "to become mature, complete, and perfect like Jesus Christ . . . Paul says that he labors with all the energy God gives him in order to present everyone perfect or mature or complete in Christ (Col 1:28–29)."[132]

---

128. Wood, "Outward Faith," 94–96.
129. Greenman, "Spiritual Formation," 23.
130. Dettoni, "Psychology of Adulthood," 15.
131. Dettoni, 15.
132. Dettoni, 15.

In summary, Dettoni concludes that spiritual formation is "an intention-al, multifaceted process which promotes the transformation by which Christ is formed in us so that we can become His continually maturing disciples."[133]

Similar to Dettoni, Dallas Willard asserts that spiritual formation is "the process of shaping our spirit" or our core being. Spiritual formation in Christ means "the process whereby the inmost being of the individual (the heart, will, or spirit) takes on the quality or character of Jesus himself." Similarly, Foster asserts that the goal of the Christian life is our "being formed, con-formed, and transformed into the image of Christ."[134] However, the spirit, heart, or will does not operate in isolation from other life aspects of a human being. Thus, Willard suggests, spiritual formation is a whole life process dealing with change in "every essential part" of a person: (1) spirit (equal to heart, or will); (2) mind (thoughts and feelings); (3) body; (4) social relations; and (5) soul.[135]

Willard also stresses that spiritual transformation involves both God's and our roles. It is "a process that involves the transformation of the whole person, that whole person must be active with Christ in the work of spiritual formation."[136] But isn't spiritual formation supposed to be based on God's grace, and not on human works? Willard replies: "Grace is not opposed to effort, it is opposed to earning [divine favor]."[137]

Greenman, in agreement with some basic principles of spiritual forma-tion that Willard and previous key authors suggest, brings the conversation further by suggesting a more comprehensive picture of spiritual formation as an alternative to an inward focus of spirituality. Greenman suggests that spiritual formation is to be understood as "our continuing response to the reality of God's grace shaping us into the likeness of Jesus Christ, through the work of the Holy Spirit, in the community of faith, for the sake of the world."[138] By saying "ongoing process," he suggests that spiritual formation

---

133. Dettoni, 16.
134. Greenman, "Spiritual Formation," 25.
135. Willard, "Spiritual Formation," 47.
136. Willard, 47.
137. Willard, 50.
138. Greenman, "Spiritual Formation," 24.

is "a lifelong journey of transformation."[139] By saying "the community of faith," he suggests that spiritual formation includes personal spiritual disciplines such as "prayer, confession, fasting and biblical meditation as well as corporate participation in the congregation's shared life of worship, fellowship and teaching." He maintains that the faith community is a communal context of spiritual formation for "mutual encouragement, mentoring, and accountability."[140]

By saying "for the sake of the world," Greenman suggests "The necessary result of spiritual formation is active participation in serving God and sharing God's work in the world."[141] A genuine spiritual formation does not merely involve loving God, but it also requires loving our neighbors as ourselves (Luke 10:27). Growing into Christlikeness does not only mean likeness in his character, but also in his mission. Thus, he suggests, "Spiritual formation at its best involves a reciprocal dynamic between gathering and scattering, contemplation and action, silence and speech, being and doing, receiving and giving."[142]

Amy Sherman personifies the Christlikeness purpose of spiritual formation through an Old Testament ideal figure of the *tsadiqqim*. "When the righteous [*tsadiqqim*] prosper, the city rejoices" (Prov 11:10). The frequent occurrences (200 times) of the word *tsaddiq* (righteous) and its plural form, *tsaddiqim*, in the Old Testament suggest its significance. N. T. Wright suggests that the meaning of "righteousness" in the Old Testament "denotes not so much the abstract idea of justice or virtue, as right standing and consequent behavior, within a community."[143] In line with this, Tim Keller also explains that most modern people tend to see the word "righteousness" in the Bible in terms of private morality, such as sexual chastity or diligence in prayer and Bible Study. However, In the Bible *tzadeqah* refers to day-to-day living in which a person conducts all relationships in family and society with fairness, generosity, and equity."[144]

---

139. Greenman, 24.
140. Greenman, 27.
141. Greenman, 27.
142. Greenman, 27.
143. Wright, "Righteousness," 590–592.
144. Keller, *Generous Justice*, 10.

Following Wright's and Keller's understanding of the Old Testament meaning of "righteousness," Sherman suggests that the "righteous" would be best understood with three dimensions or directions: up, in, and out. With this she brings the conversation of spiritual formation closer to the theme of vocational stewardship.

By "up" Sherman means the "'vertical dimension' of righteousness that involves our reverent worship of and humble dependence on God."[145] This is implied in several aspects of vocational stewardship including: (1) the purpose of work is to glorify God by serving others instead of seeking self-fulfilment as one's ultimate goal; (2) one does not fall into idolizing the job or organization for which one works; (3) there is daily reliance on the indwelling power of the Holy Spirit, and (4) one views work with an eternal perspective.

By "in" she means internal characteristics captured by phrases such as "purity in heart" and "clean hands" referring to "holy motivations and dispositions."[146] This is implied in several other aspects of vocational stewardship including: (1) maintaining personal holiness by refusing to lie, cheat, steal, or engage in a workplace sexual affair; (2) displaying the fruit of the Spirit (Gal 5:22–23) in facing difficult people or situations at the workplace; (3) generosity toward others, and (4) demonstrating compassion for the hurting and the underprivileged.

By "out" she means the social aspect of righteousness. This is implied in various expressions of vocational stewardship, such as: (1) improving conditions for the workers; (2) promoting just relations with customers, suppliers, partners, and shareholders; (3) promoting community well-being; (4) encouraging transformation within one's institution to higher standards of quality or safety or financial transparency, and (5) encouraging social reform within one's own field.

While Dettoni, Willard, and Sherman have their own ways to describe various aspects of being human, they agree on one thing: the importance of a spiritual formation that transforms the whole personhood. Willard, Greenman, and others also emphasize that spiritual formation is a life long

---

145. Sherman, *Kingdom Calling*, 47.
146. Sherman, 47.

journey. In recognition of common grace and the limitations of human inquiries in this fallen world, we will bring developmental theorists to provide
helpful insights.

Constructive-Developmental Perspectives

Developmental theories share the assumption of epigenetic principles in
which human beings are born with a genetic basis for a general pattern of
development, whether psychosocial, cognitive, moral, or faith formation.
Several key constructive-developmental theories will be presented briefly
to provide a basic framework for understanding spiritual formation from
the developmental lens: Erick Erickson, for the basic framework of human
unfolding; Jean Piaget, for the foundation of cognitive development; Robert
Kegan, for a broader theory of formation beyond childhood; Lawrence
Kohlberg, for moral development theory; Carol Gilligan, for moral decision making from a woman's point of view, and James Fowler, for the
foundational work to understand the formation of faith based on Piaget
and Kohlberg's models.[147]

Erikson relates biological development to a series of psychosocial issues
as their life tasks: (1) infancy – trust versus mistrust, (2) early childhood –
autonomy versus shame and doubt, (3) childhood (play age) – initiative
versus guilt, (4) childhood (school age) – industry versus inferiority, (5) adolescence – identity versus role confusion, (6) young adulthood– intimacy
versus isolation, (7) adulthood – generativity versus stagnation, and (8) later
adulthood – ego integrity versus despair.[148] According to Erickson there are
particular readiness and two possible developmental trajectories (positive
and negative) for each life task. He also believes that a life task worked out
in a particular stage will be continually reworked in relation to the tasks of
the following stages.[149]

Jean Piaget laid the foundation of cognitive development theory.
According to Piaget, knowing is shaped by an underlying structure of
thought as well as its particular content. Biological maturation is a necessary

---

147. Parks, *Big Questions*.

148. Erikson, *Childhood and Society*.

149. Erikson, *Life Cycle Completed*; Parks, *Big Questions*; Parret and Kang, *Teaching the Faith*.

but insufficient condition for cognitive development. It is largely influenced by the kind and quality of interaction of a person with his/her environment. Piaget suggests four age-related stages of cognitive development from infancy to adolescence: (1) the sensory-motor stage (0–2 yrs.) in which activities of the senses are coordinated with motor activities; (2) the pre-operational stage (2–7 yrs.) in which symbols and words are used to represent objects; (3) the concrete operational stage (7–11 yrs.) in which concrete objects and events are converted into abstract ideas, and (4) the formal operational stage, in which hypothetical reasoning and abstract thinking are enabled (11–13 yrs.). The formal operational age may occur up to the age of fifteen or even twenty.[150]

Parks observes that while Piaget focused his attention on the development of cognition in the individual child, other important dimensions of human becoming tend to be neglected by the Piagetians and neo-Piagetians: adulthood, emotion, being, the social process, and continuities in development. Robert Kegan[151] has effectively argued that all of these neglected factors will be embraced by taking up Piaget's central insight that "human becoming takes place in interaction between the person and his or her environment, between self and other, self and world," and thus these neglected factors "become unitary when they are gathered up in a larger conception: the transforming motion of the self-other relation which is the daily motion of life itself."[152] Kegan also argues that what has been called stages of development are merely "moments of dynamic stability – a temporary balance." He prefers to use the term "order of consciousness" to refer to a "distinct pattern of meaning-making that, evolving over time, can hold complexity with increasing adequacy."[153] Therefore, Parks concludes "Kegan has pushed Piaget theory of cognition in childhood to a broader theory of the formation of persons across time and space – a theory of the self in motion. The activity of cognition is but one actor in a larger drama: the composing of meaning. This drama has everything to do with adulthood as well as with childhood."[154]

---

150. Piaget, *Psychology of Intelligence*.
151. Kegan, "There the Dance Is"; Kegan and Lahey, *In Over Our Heads*.
152. Parks, *Big Questions*, 56.
153. Parks, 56; cf. Kegan, *In Over Our Heads*.
154. Parks, *Big Questions*, 5.

Building on Piaget's cognitive-development theory, Lawrence Kohlberg developed his seminal work on moral development theory. Some assumptions of Kohlberg's theory include (a) the primacy of moral reasoning, by which moral action can be predicted; (b) moral structure can be treated separately from moral content, and (c) two components that make up the structure of moral reasoning: perspective-taking and justice.[155] According to Kohlberg, moral development follows a pattern that can be divided into three levels, and that each level consists of two stages. Level 1 is pre-conventional, consisting of stage 1 (naïve reward orientation) and stage 2 (punishment orientation). Level 2 is conventional, consisting of stage 3 (authority orientation) and stage 4 (good boy/girl orientation). Level 3 is post-conventional, consisting of stage 5 (social contract orientation) and stage 6 (universal moral principle). Normally children are at Level 1 (pre-conventional) and adolescents reach Level 2 (conventional), while Level 3 (post-conventional) is seldom found before the age of twenty-four. However, Kohlberg's research also found that most American adults continue to use moral reasoning in Level 2, never moving into Level 3.[156]

Carol Gilligan discusses moral development through the lens of gender. Gilligan, one of Kohlberg's colleagues, found from her research that women based moral judgment on their understanding of their responsibility to care for persons. They do not seem to focus on fairness or justice as men and boys do. Kohlberg's response to this is acknowledging the need to include issues of care and responsibility in the study of moral development. He affirms that both justice and care must be addressed.[157] The debate of justice-care approaches is currently resolved empirically and conceptually, affirming care as part of the moral development theory.[158]

As Parks emphasizes, the developmental perspectives of Erikson, Piaget, Kegan, Kohlberg, and Gilligan are deeply resonant with the process of meaning-making and ordering relationships in ways that transform being, feeling, knowing, and doing. Informed by these and some other perspectives, James Fowler mapped the relationship between developmental psychologies

---

155. Kuhmerker, *Kohlberg Legacy*; Stonehouse, "Power of Kohlberg."
156. Kuhmerker, *Kohlberg Legacy*; Estep Jr., "Moral Development."
157. Stonehouse, "Power of Kohlberg," 69.
158. Sherblom, "Legacy"; Jorgensen, "Kohlberg and Gilligan."

and transformations of faith across the life span. Fowler includes evolving forms of logic, perspective taking, moral judgment, world coherence, social awareness, symbolic function, and the locus of authority as elements that influence faith development. He refers to the term "faith" as the human experience of meaning-making. Instead of focusing on the content of faith (what people believe), he focuses on the structure of faith (how people believe).[159] Faith, in Fowler's definition, has a generic meaning, regardless of religious beliefs. It is "a composing, a dynamic and holistic construction of relations that include self to others, self to world, and self to self, construed as all related to an ultimate environment . . . Faith involves both conscious and unconscious processes and holds together both rational and passional dynamics."[160] Fowler suggests a few stages through which human faith may progress: (0) primal faith (infancy); (1) intuitive/projective faith (early childhood); (2) mythic/literal faith (childhood and beyond); (3) synthetic/conventional faith (adolescence and beyond); (4) individual/reflective faith (young adulthood); (5) conjunctive faith (midlife and beyond), and (6) universalizing faith (midlife and beyond).[161]

Two major concerns have been directed toward Fowler's approach. Is it appropriate to reduce such a personal and complex experience as faith into predictable developmental stages? Does his description of the structure of his developmental progression have the universalist faith perspective as its climax?[162] However, even with these notes, Fowler's and other developmental theories have contributed to the understanding of the multiple dimensions (being, thinking, feeling, and doing) of faith that may develop through the human life span: childhood, adolescence, emerging adulthood, and all the way though adulthood.

While spiritual formation is a lifelong process,[163] the emerging adulthood period will gain more attention in the following literature review due to its importance in framing the discussion of the research findings.

---

159. Fowler, *Stages of Faith*, 99; Downs, *Teaching for Spiritual Growth*.

160. Fowler, Nipkow, and Schweitzer, *Stages of Faith*, 21.

161. Fowler, *Stages of Faith*.

162. Downs, *Teaching for Spiritual Growth*.

163. Greenman, "Spiritual Formation"; Willard, "Spiritual Formation."

Emerging Adulthood

Emerging adults, a term coined recently by Jeffrey Arnett,[164] refers to those in a ranging in age from the late teens to the late twenties,[165] or even to the early thirties.[166] In past decades educators identified this post-adolescent age period as youth, young adulthood, or simply a transition to adulthood.[167] However, as Arnett argues a radical shift in the industrialized and information society triggered by a larger enrollment in higher education and the invention of the birth control pill, have caused the younger generation in recent decades, especially the highly educated urban young, to postpone entering into marriage and parenthood, two of the key markers of adulthood.[168] Five main features mark this stage: identity exploration, instability, self-focus, feeling in-between, and the age of possibilities. This prolonged transition to adulthood, he argues, is even longer than adolescence and deserves special attention as a new life stage.[169]

Based on extensive research that initially was conducted in the context of the United States, Arnett argues that since this new life stage is influenced by cultural, socioeconomic, and other life circumstances, emerging adulthood currently exists mainly in developed countries, including Canada, most of Europe, Australia, New Zealand, the United Kingdom, some parts of Latin America, South Korea, and Japan.[170] However, some cultures in developed countries may not have this period because they encourage an earlier age for marriage and parenthood.[171] On the other hand, while median age of marriage in developing countries tends to be earlier, late teens or early twenties, young people in urban areas in those countries are also experiencing emerging adulthood because of more access to higher education and better

---

164. Arnett, "Emerging Adulthood"; *Emerging Adulthood*.

165. Arnett, *Emerging Adulthood*, 2nd ed., 7.

166. Parks, *Big Questions*, 5.

167. E.g. Merriam, Cafarella and Baumgartner, *Learning in Adulthood*; Knowles, *Modern Practice*.

168. Parks, *Big Questions*, 2–8.

169. Parks, 8–9.

170. Arnett, *Adolescence*, 12.

171. For example, young members of the Mormon Church in the United States, are encouraged to marry and begin having children early (Arnett, *Emerging Adulthood*, 2nd ed., 25).

economic conditions that allow them to postpone their adult responsibilities until the late twenties.[172]

Arnett's definition of emerging adulthood has been followed by many others since the publication of his first article fifteen years ago. However, there are also strong objections to his claim of emerging adulthood as a new developmental stage across social classes and cultures, questioning the conceptual logic as well as the sufficiency of evidence that he uses as the basis for the claim.[173] Among the questions that they ask are, "If it is a developmental stage, where did it come from epigenetically, what about it adds to human development? and in what ways are those who do not experience it . . . developmentally deficient?"[174] They argue that Arnett has mistakenly interpreted coping mechanisms of young people experiencing exploitive job situations for a freely chosen option of "identity explorations."[175]

Another objection is to the universality of Arnett's claim. The results of some empirical studies seem to challenge his claim. For example, an empirical study of a group of working class young people between seventeen and thirty in Wales[176] and another study of a group of working class people in their twenties and thirties in the United States[177] reveal that for them transition into adulthood is not primarily about self-exploration or passing economic social markers. Therefore, Cote concludes that Arnett's metanarrative "represents just some of many subjective mindsets that young people can adopt toward their prolonged transition."[178]

While the debate is not yet resolved, Sharon Daloz Parks, a well-respected developmentalist who has worked for several decades among university students, advocates convincingly for the case of emerging adulthood from a different perspective. In her *Big Questions Worthy Dreams*, she argues that the key marker for emerging adulthood is not what they do, including their

---

172. Arnett, 24–27.

173. E.g. Cote and Bynner, "Changes"; Hendry and Kloep, "Conceptualizing"; Cote, "Dangerous Myth."

174. Cote and Bynner, "Changes," 265.

175. Cote and Bynner, "Changes"; Hendry and Kloep, "Conceptualizing"; Cote, "Dangerous Myth."

176. Hendry and Kloep, "Conceptualizing."

177. Silva, "Constructing Adulthood," 510.

178. Cote, "Dangerous Myth," 182.

work, marriage, and parenthood, as this would be socio-culturally and legally diverse from one milieu to another. Rather, the key marker is "the birth of critical awareness and consequently in the dissolution and recomposition of the meaning of self, other, world, and 'God.'"[179] The importance of this stage lies in the fact that "In the process of human becoming, this task of achieving critical thought and discerning its consequences for one's sense of meaning and purpose has enormous implications for the years of adulthood to follow."[180]

While Piaget's theory explains cognitive development from infancy to adolescence, many researchers after Piaget have suggested a fifth stage that occurs in post-adolescence, taking into account a complex world of adult life, which is not counted in his formal operations stage. Several names are suggested for this stage by different scholars such as problem-finding, post-formal thinking, and dialectical thought.[181] Mackeracher argues that this developmental stage is a response to some or all of the conditions and needs of adult life such as the need to "transfer knowledge from one context to another"; the need to respond to "indeterminate situations, or ill-structured problems" which are common in work, family, and community life situations; the need to be able to deal with "uncertainties, doubts, and ambiguities"; the need to think critically in identify assumptions behind ideas or systems of ideas; and the need to deal with paradoxical situations.[182]

The claim of many researchers is that the emergence of post-formal thinking in the post-adolescent period coincides with Parks' claim of the emergence of the critical thinking capacity in emerging adulthood. This might also well correspond with the result of neuroscience research that the frontal lobe of the human brain will not fully mature until post adolescence/early adulthood (up to the age of twenty-five). This part of the brain, which is also called "the executive control center," is responsible for higher order thinking such as abstract reasoning, planning, and problem solving.[183]

---

179. Parks, *Big Questions*, 8.

180. Parks, 8.

181. Merriam and Bierema, *Adult Learning*, 183–184; Labouvie-Vief, "Emerging Structures."

182. Mackeracher, *Making Sense*, 120–121.

183. Sousa, *How the Brain*, 16–17.

Table 1. Forms of Development in Human Life[184]

	Adolescent / Conventional		Emerging Adult		Tested Adult		Mature Adult
Forms of Knowing	Authority-bound, Dualistic (tacit)	Unqualified relativism →	Probing commitment (ideological)	→	Tested commitment (systemic)	→	Convictional commitment (paradoxical)
Forms of Dependence	Dependent/ Counterdependent	→	Fragile inner-dependence	→	Confident inner-dependence	→	Inter-dependent
Forms of Community	Conventional	Diffuse →	Mentoring community	→	Self-selected class/group	→	Open to other

184. Parks, *Big Questions*, 118.

Formation in Emerging Adulthood

Based on these developmental theories and William Perry's intellectual development theory that will be presented later, Parks suggests three aspects
of faith development-forms of knowing, forms of dependence, and forms
of community – that will become a helpful framework for the discussion of
the research findings focusing on the development of vocational stewardship across different life periods with more focus on the formative years in
emerging adulthood.

Knowing and Doing

William Perry did a groundbreaking study trying to understand cognitive
development among college students. In his model he identifies sequential
positions from dualism, to relativism and ultimately to commitment in
relativism. Those who are in the dualistic position see the world in the
absolute contradiction between right or wrong and teachers are viewed as
authorities always having the right answers. As they develop, students start
to realize the possibility of more than one answer to many problems. They
become relativists depending on whether or not they are able to set criteria
for evaluating the differences among various individual perspectives and
beliefs. By the end of their college years, they realize that they have to choose
in making life decisions, and yet their commitment is open to reexamination
in the future. Perry's findings also suggest two possibilities of departure from
this progressive pattern: either "retreat" to the dualistic position or "escape"
to unqualified relativism.

The first aspect of faith development that Parks emphasizes is the "forms
of knowing." Using Perry's framework, Parks explains the transitional yet crucial stage of meaning-making in emerging adulthood. Parks modifies Perry's
nine positions of a student's relationship to knowledge into four "forms
of knowing" and adds a fifth that refers specifically to emerging adults:
(1) authority-bound/dualistic (in adolescence), in which "what a person
ultimately trusts, knows, and believes is finally based on some Authority 'out
there'";[185] (2) unqualified relativism, in which every opinion and judgment
seems to be as true and as important as any other; (3) probing commitment
(in the emerging adult), in which long lasting commitments – such as in

---

185. Parks, 72.

worldview, marriage, and career – are being explored and take their initial shapes; (4) tested commitment (in tested adult), in which "the self has a deepened quality of at-homeness and centeredness – in marked contrast to the ambivalence or dividedness of the earlier period";[186] and (5) convictional commitment (in mature adult) in which a person has a deep sense of conviction of his or her own commitment, while at the same time he or she is able to embrace paradox and a deepened capacity to hear other perspectives.

What is significant here is Parks' identification of emerging adulthood as a crucial period in which long lasting commitments are being considered and take their initial shapes. "This shift into critical reflective thought is a primary facet of becoming adult in faith and . . . a central figure of the potential of the emerging adult years."[187]

Steven Garber did research among Christian professionals in the United States who lived their faith consistently for many years after they have been graduated from college. Among the questions asked were "How does a person decide with care and commitments what will give shape and substance to life, for life? How do students learn to conscientiously connect what they believe about the world with how they live in the world?"[188] His research findings suggest that these are the people "(1) who had formed a worldview sufficient for the challenges of the modern world, (2) who had found a teacher who incarnated that worldview, and (3) who had forged friendships with folk whose common life was embedded in that worldview."[189] The first of Garber's three research findings affirms the importance of the cognitive element in the development of vocational stewardship. A robust worldview is a foundational need to build a deeply rooted integrated life in this heavily fragmented modern-postmodern world. A worldview "that will be coherent across the whole of life because it addresses the whole of life: from sexuality to politics to economics to the arts, from local commitments to global responsibilities."[190]

---

186. Parks, 92.
187. Parks, 79.
188. Garber, *Fabric of Faithfulness*, 33–34.
189. Garber, 124.
190. Garber, 138.

However, the cognitive element is just one of the various aspects of a human being. As Garber also points out later in his *Visions of Vocation*, there is always a tension between knowing and doing. "Knowing and doing are at the core of every examined life, but putting the two together is the most difficult challenge we face. At our best we long for integrity, for what we know and what we do to be coherent, because we believe they belong together intrinsically."[191] Thus, a holistic spiritual formation, as authors in the field have identified, always address the whole human dimension – whether spirit, mind, body, social relations, and soul;[192] knowledge, value system, and behavior;[193] up, in, and out.[194] Therefore, as Setran and Kiesling suggest, spiritual formation in emerging adulthood also needs to be holistic in its approach. It would include: inner transformation, costly discipleship, and embodied spiritual disciplines.

Dependence and Mentoring

The second aspect of development that Parks emphasizes is the "forms of dependence."[195] Parks suggests that affective dimension develops along with the cognitive development in the forms of dependence: (1) dependence, in which a person "depends in a primary way on the voice of a news commentator, a political leader, a celebrity, a parent, a supervisor, a religious figure, a favorite author, or a swarm of others who served as trusted mediators of Truth,"[196] followed by a period of counterdependence, which is a motion of moving apart from Authority figures "for the expansion of self into the still unknown horizon" (both take place in adolescence);[197] (2) fragile inner-dependence (in emerging adults), in which the newly gained inner dependence of a person's ability to think and decide for his or herself is accompanied by a vulnerability to failure and disappointment in a whole new horizon of opportunity and promise for his or her life; (3) confident/tested inner-dependence (in tested adults), in which a person has "a deepened

---

191. Garber, *Visions of Vocation*, 80.
192. Willard, "Spiritual Formation."
193. Dettoni, "Psychology of Adulthood."
194. Sherman, *Kingdom Calling*.
195. Parks, *Big Questions*.
196. Parks, 98.
197. Parks, 99.

capacity to compose his or her sense of value and promise and has become strong enough to let the mentor be other-even to having feet of clay";[198] and (4) interdependence (in mature adults) in which a person "most trusts the truth that emerges in the dialectic or, better, in the communion between self and other, self and the world, and self and 'God.'"[199]

Similar to the probing commitment in the cognitive dimension, the affective dimension related with the fragile inner-dependence in emerging adulthood also needs special attention in the process of meaning-making. Therefore, it does make sense that most authors addressing emerging adulthood share a common concern about the crucial role of a mentor in this period.[200]

Mentoring, in its classic sense, can be defined as "an intentional and appropriately reciprocal relationship between two individuals, a younger and older, wiser figure who assists the younger person in learning the ways of life."[201] Dunn and Sundene underline the need to develop relational rhythms of discernment, intentionality, and reflection between the disciple and the disciple rather than focusing on a set of curriculum to be transferred.[202] Setran and Kiesling underline the dual role of a mentor for emerging adults "to envision and model adult belief and responsibility" and "bringing them to a sense of continual and humble reliance on the work of God in and around them" through fostering attentiveness to God's work in the past, present, and future.[203] Parks highlights key roles of a mentor for emerging adults: "recognition, support, challenge, and inspiration – in ways that are accountable to the life of the emerging adult."[204]

Looking at these, not surprisingly, we can also find the vital role of a mentor in Garber's research on the development of vocational stewardship in the college years. "As I listened to the voices of those who still believe in a co-herent world and possibility of a coherent life, another characteristic – after

---

198. Parks, 109.

199. Parks, 113.

200. E.g., Parks, *Big Questions*; Dunn and Sundene, *Shaping the Journey*; Setran and Kiesling, *Spiritual Formation*.

201. Parks, *Big Questions*, 165.

202. Dunn and Sundene, *Shaping the Journey*.

203. Setran and Kiesling, *Spiritual Formation*, 238.

204. Parks, *Big Questions*, 167.

the forming of a worldview – was that they found a mentor during their university years whose wisdom and experience gave flesh and bone to the notion of "the good life" which was developing in the student's heart and mind."[205] These mentors may or may not be in the pulpit or classroom. "Professors, professionals, pastors all served as older friends whose cares and commitments incarnated the substance of the worldview which the student was learning to embrace."[206] The vital role of a mentor-model in developing vocational stewardship is reemphasized in his later book *The Vision of Vocation*: "Moral meaning is always learned in apprenticeship, in seeing over-the-shoulder and through-the-heart of those who have gone before us, of those who have something to teach us . . . Books are a gift, but they can never teach us to live. We have to see the words made flesh."[207]

Regarding models, Stanley and Clinton suggest mentoring could be divided into several types:[208] (1) intensive: discipler, spiritual guide, and coach; (2) occasional: counselor, teacher, and sponsor, and (3) passive: model. They suggest that within the context of Christian life, there are two types of models: a contemporary model, "a living, personal model for life, ministry, or profession who is not only an example but also inspires emulation" and a historical model, "a past life that teaches dynamic principles and values for life, ministry and/or profession."[209] While the existence and importance of models in spiritual formation is affirmed here, two notes should be made. First, in contrast to Garber's finding that mentor and model could present in one person, Stanley and Clinton suggest an either/or existence. Second, considering the different ways or relationships (two ways in mentoring, and one way in modeling), we should ask whether the inclusion of model as a type of mentoring is appropriate.

Community

The third aspect of faith development that Parks outlined is the "forms of community."[210] Parks argues "our location and social milieu (including

---

205. Garber, *Fabric of Faithfulness*, 143.

206. Garber, 143.

207. Garber, *Visions of Vocation*, 103.

208. Stanley and Clinton, *Connecting*.

209. Stanley and Clinton, 42.

210. Parks, *Big Questions*.

cyberspace) play a central role in the formation of meaning, purpose and faith."[211] She proposes corresponding forms of community that nourish the cognitive and affective development from adolescence to adulthood as: (1) conventional community (in adolescence), in which, corresponding to the Authority-bound form of cognition, community is marked by uncritical conformity to the group norms and interests; (2) mentoring community (in emerging adulthood), which "offers hospitality to the potential of the emerging adult self, poses challenging questions, and provides access to worthy dreams of self and world";[212] (3) self-selected class/group (in tested adult), which shares the meanings that are now consolidated in tested adults, without necessarily being ideologically compatible, and (4) open to the other (in mature adult), which is "a form of community that recognizes the other as 'truly other' yet part of a complex and differentiated whole."[213]

The crucial role of community in spiritual formation has been identified by many authors.[214] Peter Berger, a seminal thinker in sociological theory, both in his own work, *The Sacred Canopy*, and in the work that he co-authored with Thomas Luckmann, *The Social Construction of Reality*, argues that the process of a person's induction to a certain ethos occurs through a process of socialization. Socialization itself consists of three elements: externalization, objectification, and internalization. The process of externalization takes place through what he called legitimation and plausibility structures. His theory has been used by Christian educators to explain the impact of community in spiritual formation. Some Christian educators, notably Howard Bushnell, Albert Coe, Harrison Elliot, and John Westherhoff III even encouraged socialization as the main way to do Christian education. Thomas Groome gave a push back to this idea, saying that since the world where we live is a fallen world and the church is also not perfect, Christian education should include teaching people for critical reflection. In this way, Christians are enabled to choose among competing ideas and values for their

---

211. Parks, 115.

212. Parks, 121.

213. Parks, 131.

214. E.g. Setran and Kiesling, *Spiritual Formation*; Parks, *Big Questions*; Groome, *Christian Religious Education*.

own spiritual growth, and fulfill the task of transformation of social reality and the ongoing reformation of the church.

Setran and Kiesling identify encapsulation theory and the "matrix of transformation" theory as useful in understanding the process of identity formation in emerging adulthood.[215] Encapsulation theory argues that people commonly change through a process of socialization within a group setting, whether physically, socially, or ideologically. In other words, "Identity formation and consolidation is almost always fostered by settings in which communal relationships and practices shape meaning systems and plausibility structures, strengthening commitment along the way."[216]

Lewis Rambo identifies four components of faith community that serve as the "matrix of transformation:"[217] relationships, rituals, rhetoric, and roles. These components can be explained further as (1) a relational process serving as a transformation agent through connecting individuals to the Christian community; (2) rituals are repeating actions that strengthen identifications, serving as continual reminders of the focus of faith, and inculcating meanings beyond cognitive understanding; (3) rhetoric referring to teaching, song, and dialogue to shape the conceptual and emotional aspects, and (4) active roles through various ministry responsibilities often resulting in personal transformation.

Setran and Kiesling in recognition that identity formation takes place in every phase of the life span, suggest the "particular poignancy in emerging adulthood, when the previous bulwarks of identity – families, schools, churches, and friends – may no longer be present . . . emerging adults need mentors and communities that will provide biblical guidance while also helping them to internalize their beliefs and truths."[218]

Parks also points the specific need for community in spiritual formation in emerging adulthood. She argues that a single mentoring relationship would not be sufficient to help emerging adults to navigate through such a complex transitional phase in emerging adulthood. She suggests that only a mentoring community will be suitable for that task. Parks acknowledges

---

215. Setran and Kiesling, *Spiritual Formation*.
216. Setran and Kiesling, 75.
217. Rambo, *Understanding Religious Conversion*, 103–108.
218. Setran and Kiesling, *Spiritual Formation*, 79.

that most, if not all, mentoring research and writing since the 1970s has focused on the model of "one mentor, one protégé."[219] However, she argues "a network of belonging that serves emerging adults as a mentoring community may offer a more powerful learning and social milieu and play a critical role in the formation of meaning, purpose, and faith."[220]

In harmony with this idea, one of Garber's findings also point to the role of community in the development of the vocational stewardship of his interviewees. "From the most sophisticated cultural critiques to the street-level despair of the 'dissed' generation, the evidence seems conclusive: for individuals to flourish they need to be part of a community of character, one which has a reason for being that can provide meaning and coherence between the personal and public worlds."[221]

Parks identifies some features of the mentoring environment as a network of belonging: big-enough questions, encounters with otherness, key images-vision, a community of practice (hearth, table, and commons), and development of fruitful habits of mind "that make it possible for emerging adults to hold diversity and complexity, to wrestle with moral ambiguity, and to develop deeper wells of meaning, purpose, and faith."[222]

The influence of community could also be perceived from a wider perspective. Urie Bronfenbrenner, in his *Ecology of Human Development*, contends that human development is influenced by a person's social contexts, nested as an ecosystem. The smallest system that directly influences a person is called a microsystem. Slightly beyond a microsystem is mesosystem, consisting of several microsystems influencing a person's development. Children's mesosystems may include their family, church, and school. A mutually supporting relationship among those microsystems would promise healthier child development. Beyond mesosystem is the exosystem, social contexts that significantly but indirectly influence children through their significant others, including their father's workplace, their pastor's church denomination, and their teacher's university. The larger and further influence than the exosystem come from children's macrosystems, cultural influences that

---

219. Parks, *Big Questions*, 174.

220. Parks, 174.

221. Garber, *Fabric of Faithfulness*, 159.

222. Parks, *Big Questions*, 185.

include cultural values, socio-political conditions, and economic patterns. Across time, the child's environments also change. This is called chronosystem, that includes generational and societal changes.[223]

Learning in Adulthood

The previous section has provided insights to understand formation for vocational stewardship, particularly in the emerging adulthood period. However, as Willard, Greenman, and Dettoni, among others, suggest, formation is a life-long process, including in the years of adulthood.[224] To understand better of formation in adulthood, a brief discussion on theories of learning in adulthood will be presented in this section. It includes Knowles' Andragogy, Freire's Dialogue and Praxis, and Groome's Shared Praxis approach.

Andragogy

The concept of andragogy promoted by Malcolm Knowles is one of the most important pieces of the mosaic that has influenced the field of adult education for more than forty years. From each of Knowles' assumptions numerous implications can be developed for the design, implementation, and evaluation of adult learning activities.[225]

The term *andragogy* means "the art and science of helping adults learn," in contrast to pedagogy, "the art and science of teaching children."[226] Andragogy is based on a set of assumptions which Knowles contrasted to pedagogical assumptions.[227]

1. The need to know: Adults need to know the benefit of learning a certain thing before they learn it, while children only need to know that they must learn to pass an exam.

2. The learner's self-concept: Adults are self-directing human beings, while children are dependents.

3. The role of experience: Adults come into learning activities with a growing reservoir of experience as a source for learning, while

---

223. Balswick and King, *Reciprocating Self*; Parrett and Kang, *Teaching the Faith.*
224. Willard; Greenman; Dettoni.
225. Merriam and Bierema, *Adult Learning.*
226. Knowles, *Modern Practice*, 40, 42.
227. Knowles, Holton, and Swanson, *Adult Learner*, 59–69; Knowles, *Modern Practice*, 43–44.

in the pedagogical model the experience of their teachers and textbook writers is much more important to the child as the resource for learning.

4. Readiness to learn: Adults' readiness to learn is closely related to their need to cope with real-life situations, particularly when they move from one developmental stage to the next. Children are assumed to be ready to learn when they need to pass, based on age-level and standardized curriculum.

5. Orientation to learning: Adult learning is life-centered (task-centered or problem-centered), while in pedagogy learning is acquiring subject-matter content.

6. Motivation: Adults are more motivated to learn by internal motivators (such as job satisfaction, self-esteem, and quality of life), while children are motivated by external motivators (such as grades, teacher's approval, and parental pressures).

There was a shift, however, in Knowles' thought about the relationship between the two models. This is based on the feedback that children and youth seemed to learn better in many circumstances when some elements of the andragogical model were applied. On the other hand, he also found that there were situations where the andragogical model did not work well for adult learners.[228] Hence, the andragogical model is not perceived to be unique for adults anymore. Rather, the appropriate model depends on the learning situation. The pedagogical model might be more workable for adult learners when they encounter a totally new learning area.[229] Knowles' later position can be summarized as "that pedagogy-andragogy represents a continuum ranging from teacher-directed to student-directed learning and that both approaches are appropriate with children and adults, depending on the situation."[230] This does not, however, eliminate the basic assumption that in most situations the andragogical model is more workable for adult learners.

The transformative learning theory introduced by Mezirow,[231] after much research, controversy, and development, has currently surpassed andragogy

228. Merriam and Bierema, *Adult Learning*.
229. Knowles, Holton, and Swanson, *Adult Learner*, 68.
230. Merriam, Caffarella, and Baumgartner, *Learning in Adulthood*, 87.
231. Mezirow, *Education*.

and provided a new identity for the field of adult education.[232] However, Merriam and Bierema are still optimist about the influence of andragogy. "Despite the lack of research documenting the assumptions of andragogy, and despite the criticism that it ignores the sociocultural context of learning, andragogy continues to be a major theory/mode/approach to understanding and planning instruction for adult learners."[233] Therefore, recognizing the usefulness of andragogy for a better understanding of adults as adult learners, it will also be used as one of the resources to frame the discussion on relevant research findings.

Dialogue and Praxis

Another important resource for adult learning is Freire's approach. According to Freire, dialogue is the heart of a humanizing pedagogy. Conviction is not something that an educator can simply give to a learner. It is a result of the learner's own *conscientizaqao,* consciousness raising.[234] In dialog learners are treated as subjects with whom the educator works together to understand reality and re-create knowledge through their joint reflection and action. With this approach the learner's involvement will be "not pseudo-participation, but committed involvement."[235] Therefore, Freire rejects the commonly practiced "banking education," through which ideas and information are "deposited" by the educator into the mind of the learners. Instead he suggests "problem-posing education" through which learners are stimulated to develop critical reflection about their own social problems.[236]

Freire also stresses the importance of both reflection and action in adult learning. Without action, reflection will only end in "verbalism," empty words that do not change anything in real life. Without reflection, action will end in merely "activism," having superficial meaning and making dialogue impossible. It is the praxis, the continuing cycle of action and reflection, that he argues have the liberating power to transform the world.[237]

---

232. Taylor and Cranton, "Transformative Learning Theory."
233. Merriam and Bierema, *Adult Learning*, 58.
234. Freire, *Pedagogy*, 54.
235. Freire, 56.
236. Freire, 66.
237. Freire, 75–76.

Influenced by Freire, Thomas Groome introduces a shared praxis approach, an excellent method for Christian religious education that starts with the participants' experience.[238] There are five steps, called movements, in this approach: (1) naming present action, (2) critical reflection on present action, (3) making accessible Christian Story and Vision, (4) dialectical hermeneutics to appropriate Story/Vision to participants' story and visions, and (5) decision/response for lived Christian faith.[239] A "generative theme" is chosen before the movements as a focus or context of reflection and discussion during the shared learning process. The combination of critical reflection, praxis, and dialogue in this approach make it potentially beneficial for fostering the development of vocational stewardship in Christian workers.

Summary of Precedent Literature

Precedent literature in this chapter has provided a theoretical framework for researching the development of vocational stewardship among Indonesian Christian professionals. The first two sections of the literature review focused on the theology of work, theology of mission, and faith at work movement. It provided a framework to understand the context and significance of the research. The last section of the review focused on theories relevant with formation in emerging adulthood and later years of adulthood. It provided a framework to explore the meaning and significance of the research findings by taking into account both the process of and factors influencing the development of vocational stewardship. A dialectical interaction between precedent literature and the research findings will be explored in chapter 5.

---

238. Although there were pros and cons, the shared praxis approach has gained wide acceptance across various Christian traditions (see Horell, "Thomas Groome").

239. There are slight modifications of the fourth and fifth movements in Groome's *Sharing Faith*, from the ones in his previous work, *Christian Religious Education*, in which the fourth movement is the dialectical hermeneutic between Story and participant's stories and the fifth movement is between Vision and participant's visions.

CHAPTER 3

Methods

Research Design

This study was conducted with the basic or interpretive type of a qualitative research. According to Merriam there are four key characteristics of qualitative research: "the focus is on process, understanding, and meaning; the researcher is the primary instrument of data collection and analysis; the process is inductive; and the product is richly descriptive."[1] A central characteristic of qualitative research is that "individuals construct reality in interaction with their social worlds," in which meaning "is not discovered but constructed,"[2] Thus, this research focused on the lens of Indonesian Christian professionals as they construct meaning of their experiences in developing vocational stewardship.

The purpose of this study was to explore the personal development of vocational stewardship among Indonesian Christian professionals.

The Research Questions guided the study were:

1. How do Indonesian Christian professionals describe their vocational stewardship?
2. How do Indonesian Christian professionals describe the significance of their college years for the development of their vocational stewardship?
3. How do Indonesian Christian professionals describe the personal development of vocational stewardship after their college years?

---

1. Merriam, *Qualitative Research*, 14.
2. Merriam, 22.

Population and Sample Selection

The population for this study was Indonesian Christian professionals who have university/college education backgrounds and worked in a variety of full time or part time paid work. For this qualitative data, sample selection is based on the purposive or purposeful sampling strategy, instead of probability sampling.[3] "Since generalization in a statistical sense is not a goal of a qualitative research, probabilistic sampling is not necessary nor even justifiable in qualitative research."[4] Purposeful sampling is "based on the assumption that the investigator wants to discover, understand, and gain insight and therefore must select a sample from which the most can be learned."[5]

The sample consisted of twenty-eight participants, who lived and worked in Indonesia. Participants to be interviewed were selected with the following considerations:

1. Recognizing various possible "pathways" of vocational stewardship, participants were selected based on their daily work as Christian professionals. Compared to other "pathways" such as volunteering their skill outside their daily work, this "pathway" is considered as "the primary and most important avenue for deploying vocational power."[6]

2. Selecting participants based on their good reputation in their work and their clear faith commitment.

3. Selecting participants who had sufficient working experience as the basis for their reflection. The youngest participant had eight years working experience due to the potentially rich data that she could provide. All the other participants had at least ten years working experience when they were interviewed.

4. Attempting to enhance transferability of the study with maximum variation,[7] by considering several elements such as types of work, age related with length of work experience, gender, and campus ministry experience.

---

3. Patton, Qualitative Research; Merriam, *Qualitative Research*.
4. Merriam, *Qualitative Research*, 77.
5. Merriam, 77.
6. Sherman, *Kingdom Calling*, 144.
7. Merriam, *Qualitative Research*, 227–228.

Description of Participants

Of the twenty-eight participants, sixteen are male and twelve are female. The ages of participants in this study ranged from the thirties to sixties, with almost half of them (thirteen out of twenty-eight) in their forties. This means that there is a spectrum of work experiences as the basis of reflection on their vocational journey from the freshest of one decade to the longest of over four decades of work. This means that they also differ in generation.

Table 2. Age of Participants in the Study

Age of Participants	Frequency
30 – 39	6
40 – 49	13
50 – 59	6
60 – 69	3

Most participants (nineteen) lived and worked in Jakarta, the capital of Indonesia, one of the most favorite cities that draws new college graduates from different parts of the country to work. Five participants lived and worked in two satellite cities of Jakarta. The remaining four participants lived and worked in Bandung, one of the centers for higher education, located 150 km from Jakarta.

The highest number of participants completed their college degree in Jakarta (eleven participants) and Bandung (eleven participants). The remaining completed their college degree in other cities in Indonesia (five participants) and in the United States (one participant). Eight participants also have master's degrees, not all of them in the same field as their undergraduate degree. Two participants have their doctorate degree.

Participants' majors for their college degree included engineering (ten), economy/business (five), law (four), medical (three), tourism (two), agriculture (two), psychology (one), and journalism (one). Their work field also varies: industrial management (production, consultant), homebuilding (private company, non-profit organization), business (business owner, director, auditor, banking), politics (non-profit organization, politician), education (university professor, high school teacher, and teachers' trainer), medical (general practitioner, ophthalmologist, and internist), tourism (hotel manager), law (lawyer, prosecutor, and bureaucracy), journalism (journalist). A quick cross check between the college education and work field would indicate that participants' work field does not necessarily correspond with their major in college.

Participants' work distribution could also be viewed as a private company, state-owned company, government institution, and non-profit organization. Two participants who previously worked as Christian professionals, but at the point of interview had spent a significant period of time to be home makers, were also included as participants, to provide a nuance of calling within the family life context.

Three quarters (twenty-one out of twenty-eight) of the participants had significant involvement with campus ministries when they were in college, with a range of participation in their campus fellowship groups, including active participation in their fellowship group meetings and undertaking various ministry and leadership responsibilities in their group. The remaining seven participants had no contact or little contact with campus ministry when they were in college. Most of their influence in college life came from their church involvement.

Social and Religious Context of Christian Professionals in Indonesia

Social Context

Indonesia is an archipelago, composed of 13,677 islands, of which around 1,000 are inhabited. The country stretches about 3,400 miles from east to west, and about 1,000 miles from north to south. Population of Indonesia in 2015 is around 250 million inhabitants.[8] 60 percent of Indonesian populations live in Java, the fifth largest island in the country, where Jakarta, the capital of Indonesia, is located.

Indonesia is culturally and religiously diverse. Among the largest tribes, which have their own cultures, are Javanese, Sundanese, Madurese,

---

8. BPS Indonesia 2014, "Proyeksi Penduduk menurut Provinsi, 2010–2035." Badan Pusat Statistik Indonesia. Accessed 17 October 2016.

Minangkabau, Batak, Bali, Bugis, Aceh, Riau, Sasak, Toraja, Chinese, and Papua peoples. The composition of the Indonesian population in 2010 based on religion is Islam (87.18%), Protestant (6.96%), Catholic (2.91%), Hindu (1.69%), Buddhist and Confucius (0.77%), and unspecified (0.41%).[9]

Higher education is still a privilege in this country. Enrollment in tertiary education is 2.25 percent of the total population.[10] Only 5.23 percent of the population have completed higher education of at least a one-year program. The number becomes 3.34 percent when the lowest is four-year college program.[11]

Among the biggest challenges that this country faces are poverty, related with a large inequality in income distribution,[12] corruption (in 2015 rank 88 out of 168 country),[13] and latent inter-religious tensions.

Christianity in Indonesia

Christianity came to Indonesia as early as in the sixteenth century. The first Catholic missionaries arrived with the Portuguese in Moluccas, the eastern part of the archipelago, in 1522. By the 1590s there were over fifty thousand Roman Catholics in Moluccas. Protestant Christianity was brought in to Indonesia by Dutch missionaries as early as 1599. Within several decades, Dutch Reformed churches spread in various port cities in the archipelago. Different mission agencies came from the Netherlands during the colonial era. The results were that Reformed churches spread throughout the archipelago. It became the largest denomination after Indonesia got its independence in 1945. Other denominations were brought in from other European countries and the United States to Indonesia in the nineteenth century (Lutheran) or twentieth century (including Pentecostal and CMA).[14]

Christianity in Indonesia is spread throughout the country. The population of Christians differs from one area to another. In one province,

9. BPS Indonesia 2010, "Sensus Penduduk 2010: Penduduk Menurut Kelompok Umur and Agama yang Dianut." Badan Pusat Statistik Indonesia. Accessed 17 October 2016, http://sp2010.bps.go.id/index.php/site/tabel?tid=320danwid=0.

10. Knoema, "Number of Students."

11. BPS Indonesia 2010.

12. World Bank, "Indonesia."

13. Transparency International, *Corruption*.

14. End Harta Dalam; Ragi Carita 1; Ragi Carita 2.

the Christian population can reach as high as 88 percent, while in other provinces it can be as low as 0.5 percent.[15] Christianity in Indonesia consists of diverse denominational groups. The four largest denominations are Reformed, Catholic, Lutheran, and Pentecostal, followed by denominations with fewer members including Christian and Missionary Alliance, Baptist, Adventist, and Methodist. The division between ecumenical churches and evangelical churches in Indonesia is not as strict as in some other countries. This is particularly true at the level of church members. Many church members of ecumenical churches retain their membership and serve in their church while they are also affiliated with evangelical parachurch organizations. However, until recently the division is still more apparent in the level of church leadership and organization.

Ecumenical churches in Indonesia joined in PGI, the National Fellowship Council of Churches in Indonesia, founded in 1950, five years after Indonesian independence. In 2005 its membership included eighty-one out of three hundred church organizations in Indonesia, although in terms of membership, it consisted of over half of the Protestants in Indonesia. Evangelical churches in Indonesia joined in PII, Indonesian Evangelical Council, founded in 1971. Pentecostal churches mostly are members of the Communion/Council of Pentecostal Churches in Indonesia, founded in 1979.[16]

The Student Movement in Indonesia had its seed as early as 1928, two decades before Indonesian independence. A World Student Christian Federation (WSCF) conference in 1933 took place in Jakarta, and a local student group CSV of Java, was accepted as a member of WSCF. In 1954 it became GMKI, Indonesian Christian Student Movement. Many of its leaders became prominent leaders in the ecumenical movement.[17] Evangelical campus ministries, including Perkantas (affiliated to IFES), Navigators, LPMI (Campus Crusade), and charismatic student ministries grew from early 1970 onwards as the influence of GMKI in campuses declined.[18]

---

15. BPS Indonesia 2010.
16. Aritonang and Steenbrink, *History of Christianity*.
17. Aritonang and Steenbrink, 828.
18. Sasongko et al., *Kisah yang*.

Campus fellowship groups can be found in almost every major city throughout the country where higher education in college level exists. Among their activities are weekly large group meetings, small groups that function as growth groups, retreats, student leader training, and regional and national conferences. Most Indonesian Christian professionals who were involved in campus ministry experienced formation within these campus fellowship groups during their college years. The national network was often beneficial for them in their post-college years, since many of them commonly moved to another city to work. Graduate fellowship groups formed in various cities became a helpful network of belonging, particularly as they transitioned into the new living environment in another city.[19]

Data Collection

Data collection was conducted within the span of three months from the end of May through mid-August of 2015. More than half of the participants were selected from a list of workshop speakers for mission through profession in a national conference for student leaders, held by a parachurch organization. The rest were recruited from personal knowledge of the researcher and recommendations from "informal gate keepers."[20]

Potential participants were contacted by email and/or phone and asked for their availability for interviews.[21] Data collection was conducted with approximately sixty minutes of semi-structured interviews for each participant. The interviews were guided by a list of protocol questions, but no predetermined wording or order strictly applied.[22] Most interviews were conducted in Jakarta (nineteen) and two satellite-cities (five). The remaining (four) were conducted in Bandung, 150 km from Jakarta. Most interviews were conducted at the workplace during their lunch-break hour. Due to the time constraint and distance, two interviews were conducted via Skype. One participant was doing his doctorate degree abroad at the point of data collection.

---

19. Sasongko et al.
20. Seidman, *Interviewing*, 49.
21. Merriam, *Qualitative Research*.
22. Merriam, 89.

Initially as a follow up there were one or two focus group meetings planned to function as member checks[23] and also to explore issues that came up during the preliminary analysis of the interviews.[24] However, when the data collection process was halfway done, the researcher found out that the issue of time constraint and distance made this plan unfeasible. Therefore, the plan to organize focus group discussion for the participants aborted.

Participants were asked to read and sign the informed consent as an official consent to be interviewed for the research. All interviews were recorded. Field notes were also taken. Each participant was notified that the whole interview was going to be recorded and transcribed for the purpose of research analysis.

Initially thirty participants were interviewed based on the sample selection criteria. However, during the interview process it was apparent that two participants did not sufficiently meet the criteria, indicated from the way they could not respond to the interview questions clearly, particularly on the first of the three research questions. Therefore, after doing a recheck on the interview transcripts, the researcher decided to drop two of the participants. Thus, the data to be analyzed was based on twenty-eight participants' responses during the interview.

Data Analysis

All interviews were transcribed with the help of three transcribers who had journalistic backgrounds. Each transcript was verified against the interview recording by the researcher. All interviews were conducted in the Indonesian language. Relevant data was translated to English as a part of this report. The transcripts of the interviews and the field notes were analyzed using HyperResearch 3.7.3.

Open coding was conducted to construct initial categories. Afterward, a comparative analysis process was conducted. The naming of the categories, sub-categories/themes, and codes came from three sources: myself as the researcher, the participants' words (in vivo codes), and the literature. Potential themes and codes were grouped to answer each research question.

---

23. Merriam, 217.
24. Morgan, *Focus Group*, 23.

The emerging categories were tested throughout the whole data so that the categories were not only "responsive to the purpose of the research," but also as "exhaustive" as possible.[25]

Transferability

Transferability refers to "the possibility of the results of a qualitative study 'transferring' to another setting."[26] I used a rich, thick description of the findings as the most common method to enhance transferability of the study.[27] Efforts to maximize transferability were also conducted with typical sampling and maximum variation.[28] Typical sampling was attempted by choosing participants who were more likely to represent the larger population of Indonesian Christian professionals, such as with the inclusion of both male and female, working in Indonesia, and some of them having campus ministry experiences. Maximum variation was attempted with the variety of the participants' background such as their type of work, age, length of work experience, male-female, and with or without campus ministry experience.

Researcher Stance

Researcher stance or researcher position is an explanation of the researcher's "biases, dispositions, and assumptions regarding the research to be undertaken" to allow readers "to better understand how the individual researcher might have arrived at the particular interpretation of the data," and also to allow the researcher's values and expectations that might influence the conduct and conclusions of the research being brought into surface.[29] For this purpose, I am offering an explanation of my stance in doing this study.

My years of involvement in campus ministry have developed my interest to understand how the discipleship process in campus ministry affects work life after graduation from college. I have listened to exciting sporadic stories of different graduates from time to time about how their college life

---

25. Merriam, *Qualitative Research*, 178–193.
26. Merriam, 227.
27. Merriam, 227.
28. Merriam, 228.
29. Merriam, 219, 220.

has prepared them for their commitment to live with their faith in their work life. From these encounters, I have a conviction that when a rigorous qualitative research on the personal development of vocational stewardship is applied to this group of people, rich information could potentially be gathered of the impact of their college life to the personal development of vocational stewardship in their work life. This background has set my interest to focus my study on the personal development of vocational stewardship among university graduates, in which the major proportion of my subjects were those who have a campus ministry background.

On the other hand, from encounters with those who entered their work life as university graduates with minimum or even without campus ministry experience, I had a conviction that the development of the vocational stewardship they experienced could potentially be different from their colleagues who had campus ministry experience. Their college years might not be the most important or foundational in their experience of developing vocational stewardship. Therefore, I believed that including them as subjects for this study would bring important nuances to the study of the personal development of vocational stewardship among university graduates. With the more holistic picture gained, I hoped that the educational insights resulted from this study would benefit a wider audience, which is the church with the diverse characteristics of its members.

Subjects were selected based on the criteria that they embody the perception and expression of the connection between their daily work and God's mission. However, the selection of the subjects was largely influenced by my theological understanding of what kind of person that would meet these criteria.

CHAPTER 4

Research Findings

The purpose of this research was to explore the personal development of vocational stewardship among Indonesian Christian professionals. The study was guided by the following research questions:

1. How do Indonesian Christian professionals describe their vocational stewardship?
2. How do Indonesian Christian professionals describe the significance of their college years for the development of their vocational stewardship?
3. How do Indonesian Christian professionals describe the personal development of vocational stewardship after their college years?

An analysis of transcripts of twenty-eight participants' interviews resulted in the identification of the following four major categories responsive to the research questions: (1) dimensions of vocational stewardship; (2) development of vocational stewardship; (3) empowering relationships for the development of vocational stewardship; and (4) empowering communities for the development of vocational stewardship. The findings described in this chapter are organized according to these four major categories and, within each category, themes that emerged regarding dimensions of and key developmental contributions toward vocational stewardship among Indonesian Christian professionals are also included.

Category-1: Dimensions of Vocational Stewardship

The first category of findings describes participants' description of their vocational stewardship experiences. Within this first major category, three themes capture the ways in which participants describe their vocational stewardship: First, the meaning of work, related to their perception on the connection between their work and God's work; second, identity as a worker, related to their sense of calling; and third, the purpose of work, related to their orientation to serve others through work accompanying their sense of calling. These three themes reflect multiple dimensions of vocational stewardship, within which can also be found conceptual and practical elements, and also cognitive, affective, and active elements.

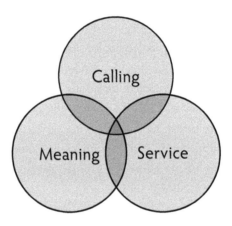

Figure 1. Dimensions of Vocational Stewardship.

Meaning of Work

The first theme of vocational stewardship is the perceived meaning of work. Commonly, participants perceive that their work is connected with God's work. Most participants view their work as intrinsically meaningful. A few of them view their work as also, or only, instrumentally meaningful.

Intrinsically Meaningful

Most participants in this study refer to the intrinsic meaning of their work. They believe their work is meaningfully connected with God's work regardless of whether their work is overtly useful as an instrument for evangelism or other religious purposes. This includes the perception that their work reflects God's character, is part of God's mission, and fulfill the biblical cultural mandate.

Work as a reflection of God's character

The first shared understanding among participants who believe that their work has intrinsic meaning is referring to their work – whether as a home builder, a politician, an auditor, or an IT worker – as a reflection of God's character (PT; MI; NC; YM). Their perceptions underscore the intrinsic meaning of various kinds of work which are commonly undervalued and labeled as perhaps "worldly" or "secular."

PT views his work as a home builder/developer, primarily helping to fulfill physical needs for people in society, as a reflection of God's creative character:

> After some time, I asked [myself], "What am I doing here?" . . .
> But I was reminded that God is the Creator. Creating what?
> God created everything. So we are also assigned here to cre-
> ate something, producing something, bringing out something.
> Developers, despite all aspects of business achievements, are
> creating a life environment for people in the future. When we
> started working, there was nothing but land. But there will be
> a living environment for many people. And after a few years,
> the environment is created.

MI asserts that his work in politics is a reflection of God's concern for justice in this world. He cites an example of how God upheld justice when Cain murdered Abel. "If God did not care, God would just let it be . . . but God cared, God acted immediately, God punished. God punished while protecting Cain as well, so that he is not murdered in return allowing anarchy to reign." Further, MI suggests that later on God also invited human beings to participate in upholding justice on earth. "When God was about to punish Sodom and Gomorrah, God involved Abraham. Then when God released the Israelites from slavery, he did not do it by himself, he sent Moses." Therefore, he concludes, "God cares about how we live together [in a society]. God wants to show his attributes, through things like that. And God wants to use human beings to uphold his justice, and when we uphold that justice we show his *Imago Dei*."

When asked about her reflections on the relationship between her work and God's work, NC, an auditor, describes how her work maintaining accurate record participates in God's plan much like safeguards help to maintain order in a company. Similarly, YM articulates his reflections on his IT systems work as a reflection of God's orderly character:

> God is an orderly God, thus, when we make it orderly, achieving its supposed potentials, we're doing our part in bringing the kingdom of God into this world . . . In terms of efficiency, affectivity, orderliness, God wants it to operate well, not with many frictions nor brokenness. One of the strengths of IT here is to give integration, bridging brokenness, silo, so people can work together better and support each other. [Where] there is a connection, there are relationships. Those are the things that we facilitate.

TB, a seasoned businessman, emphasizes an additional dimension regarding the perception of work as a reflection of God's character. TB helps migrant workers, ex-prostitutes, and lepers by providing entrepreneur training for them, and he reflects that what he does is a reflection of God's compassion to the underprivileged and the outcast. He comments on an experience when a prototype entrepreneur class was conducted to help a group of ex-prostitutes, ex-pimps, and impacted community members in one area:

> There were ten ex-pimps and ex-prostitutes, and sixteen others. They did not tell us. They kept it from us. But over time, I knew who were prostitutes [and] who were not. As a Christian, I was honored to meet people whom our Lord Jesus loves. I ate together with them. I sat together with them. And I know my Lord will do the same. And not everyone has the same opportunity that I had. [The opportunity] to be able to eat and sit with them, talk with them. To me that's a blessing.

For TB, teaching entrepreneurship to these outcasts was intrinsically meaningful as a reflection of God's love and concern for them. Recognizing their work as an extension of God's hands in this world enabled TB and the other participants to work meaningfully and wholeheartedly.

Work as part of God's mission

The second common understanding of an intrinsic meaning of work, shared by one third of the participants, is the perception that their work is part of

God's mission in the world. They believe that the scope of biblical mission is not limited to only verbal gospel proclamation or religious work. With a larger perspective on the scope of Christ's redemptive work, they believe that God's mission includes all spheres of life and is therefore accomplished through all kinds of work. As MM, a hotel manager, asserts, "People often say that mission means going to remote areas. People tend to understand it that way. But in my opinion, mission could be anywhere God placed us. That's our mission field. We don't always have to go to the jungle . . . Marketplace is our mission field, and we have our own difficulties over there."

This understanding of the larger scope of biblical mission helps significantly in making sense behind the meaning of professional work as well as their search for God's calling on their life. YM recalls how this understanding became a starting point for his own discovery: "I started the discovery of my calling at the National Student Conference in 1995. In that conference [two panel discussion speakers] talked about mission . . . I learned that mission is not limited to ministry." Later on, in the same conference, this understanding was affirmed when a highly respected senior pastor gave an altar call. In it the pastor stressed the point that "a calling to submit as God's servant does not always translate into being a full-time [religious] worker."

Similarly, RT recalls that he initially understood "mission was going somewhere [to preach] the gospel." It was his mentor, a foreign missionary, who helped him to grasp a more holistic understanding of mission, saying to him: "God wants you as a professional to go into your field. It was no accident that God put you in ITB, a prestigious school. God will use your professionalism to address corruption problems. Fight it from inside! We can't just talk from the outside! she said. We need to get inside!" This insight was crucial in his vocational journey. He recalls, "That made me stop discriminating." He knew that he was "doing mission" when working as an electrical engineer. "That gave me a strong passion [to work]!"

Beyond what we do for other human beings, CT also argues that biblical mission includes the responsibility of caring for the environment. He insists that "when Christ redeems us, he's not just redeeming us as human beings. But, he also redeems our relationship with nature." This comprehensive nature of Christ's redemption, he argues, is based on the understanding of the multidimensional impact of sin. "When Adam and Eve fell into sin, the relationship between human beings and God was broken. The relationship between human beings was also broken, severed. The relationship between human beings and the creation was also damaged. When this relationship between human beings and creation is broken, people exploit and damage nature." Therefore, he concludes, "our responsibility is not just to heaven. We live in this world. We also need to maintain our environment. With my experience wrestling with environmental issues, I'm becoming more convinced that this is our responsibility."

Related to God's mission to restore the fallen world, some participants also view the connection between their work and God's work in their role of bringing the biblical values of a restored humanity into their workplace or through their work. They stress that it is important that these biblical values are expressed in lived values, not in merely religious ceremonies or rituals (HC, WI). The spheres may vary. For some participants, it was the company values, whether as owners, managers, or team leaders (TS; RB; TG; SE; NC). For others, it was in society (public virtue vs. private virtue), including through politics, law, the role of a counselor, and educator (MI; RI; LT; TO), and also in the family (WO; GT).

Work as part of the biblical cultural mandate

A third shared understanding among participants who perceive their work as intrinsically meaningful is an understanding that it is an integral part of the cultural mandate given at creation (Gen 1:28). They view their work, whether as a scholarly researcher, a physician, or an IT expert (CT, DC, YM) as part of the larger cultural mandate. DC shared his story when he was an undergraduate: "A friend brought me to [a church]. There, my eyes were opened to the fact that we have a gospel mandate and a cultural mandate. [I learned] that we are not just to fulfill the gospel mandate. [I learned that] we also have a responsibility to the cultural mandate, to influence all facets of life." Without undermining the significance of the gospel mandate (Matt 28:29–20), they perceive the importance of both the cultural and gospel mandates. CT, for example, says that "these two will go side-by-side" in his role as a faculty member.

Instrumentally Meaningful

A number of participants also perceive an instrumental meaning of their work for the ministry of the gospel. This includes the perception that their work or expertise is a way to support the ministry of the gospel, a platform to share the gospel, and the notion that a Christian worker is an "opened letter of Christ." Within this group, however, there are two types of participants: those who view their work as having both intrinsic and instrumental meaning, and those who view that their work as purely instrumental.

My work is meaningful in its support to the ministry of the gospel

A few participants found their work meaningful through an understanding that their work or expertise supports the ministry of the gospel. For example, for PT, his work as a homebuilder is meaningful since through his work he can provide sites for churches to worship in the new neighborhood that his company developed.

> When I built those shop-houses, I did not know that there would be a church in that place. In the middle of the night, as I was waiting for a casting work to arrive, I prayed, "Lord, why did You put me to work here? What am I building? This is just for the world." But when the project was completed, churches popped up there. "Oh, so that was it! Oh Lord, I was just providing [the building]."

This instrumental meaning of work, however, is accompanied by a reflection on an intrinsic meaning of his work. In other part of the interview he said that his work as a home builder/developer is meaningful since in creating a new neighborhood his work reflects God's character as Creator.

Slightly different from PT, WO's perception on the meaning of her work tends to be purely instrumental. The tendency to divide between religious and non-religious works can be indicated in her statement such as: "A company's vision is only to get profit in the end. How about churches', non-profit institution's visions? To me, it's more noble, soulful, embracing the community!" Her further statement seems to strengthen this sacred-secular perspective:

> I had to work to support [my husband] economically because it was the start of his work. But once that's passed, I think it

was more important for me to eventually be more focused on children, on family. I have no regret whatsoever to leave my career because I knew that my life is beyond just gaining money, I don't [want to] live just to pursue a career . . . If God gave me knowledge, all kinds of experiences, they're for my family, for life. I live not for money. I need money to live. But once I have it, it's enough. It's something vain, not eternal. What is more eternal than that? I choose the eternal one.

Work meaningful as platform to share gospel

Several participants assert that their work is connected to God's work since it serves as a platform to share the gospel (TO; NQ; RB). TO, a high school teacher, claims that he is able to share biblical values even through teaching mathematics:

> I found a lot of connection between Math and Religion. I could even bring the gospel through the scope of Math. When I teach about limits, for example. Subject matter of limit. I'd tell the kids, "Now kids, after we learn about limit, there are two kinds of numbers in this world. One is a constant, like my age. I could be fifty, or sixty. It's a constant, definite. And the other one is indefinite number, indefinite only belongs to God, it's eternal. I told them so. My question is what if a constant limit is divided by an infinite [number]? If they answer zero, "You're right, the answer is zero. Because if we live by only prioritizing human values, then there is nothing, the value is zero." (Laugh) Now I ask again, "what if infinite limit [number] divided by constant?" "It's infinite, Sir." "Good. So, if your thinking and attitude gives you eternal values, you will have eternal values." Then I say, in my belief, Jesus said that whoever believes him will live even though he is dead. This raises a lot of questions and there were discussions afterward.

For NQ, her medical profession and the ministry of the gospel go hand-in-hand. Since an early assignment to serve a remote area when she was a young physician, this has been true:

I was assigned to a remote area, and was so ready even though there was a heated conflict between the district chief and the doctor who served before me. An assassination almost happened. I was able to clarify the situation and had prayer meetings with the people, serving local churches. I was there for three years. After the first year, I moved to another local clinic. I also started prayer meetings [in the new place]. Mostly I set up a Bible camp for Sunday school children . . . That helped me to not to get bored working in the local clinic. Since then I have conducted Bible camps, women's retreats, served in church every Sunday, and have also served villages by providing medicine. I first lead a worship service and then distribute medications [to the people].

NQ also stresses that the workplace is a place to be a witness for the gospel. "In alumni Bible Studies I often said . . . God does not place us haphazardly. You were put where you are in your profession. God has a plan. Don't complain that it's only a place to make money. We are put there to be witnesses, to look for souls, to color people around us. I always say that in Alumni Bible Study."

In his business, RB works with non-Christian colleagues and employees. He recalls that gaining the trust of long-term colleagues by investing in healthy work relationships enables him to go deeper into conversations about faith. "In many things, I have opportunities to talk about my faith. Sometimes I tell them, for us, it's like this." However, RB did not perceive this instrumental meaning of work as the sole or the main purpose of his work with non-Christians. In other parts of his interview he repeatedly emphasized his conviction that God has called him to help low-educated people by providing decent job opportunities for them. The opportunities to share his faith with his colleagues and workers appeared as parts of normal daily life conversations within years of working together with them.

Work meaningful as living testimony

Other participants find meaning in their work since they view it as a living testimony for Christ (IT; BU; PK). They highlight that a Christian worker is "an open letter," implying a living testimony of Christ through all that one lives and does (2 Cor 3:2–3). As a physician, IT shares her conviction, "To me, we are like open letters. I mean, we cannot share the gospel openly. We couldn't. Could we? But hopefully, by being a slightly better doctor, the slight difference will be evocative." Similarly, BU perceives the connection between his work and God's work centered in his role as God's witness as a banker. "More about witnessing. That's what I always think. Not just to make money. Yes, money is important for the family. But the definition of glorifying God through work is what we talked about earlier. Setting an example, [to express that] Christians are like this. Different!" They believe that the living testimony of their deeds is not a replacement for the verbal sharing of the gospel message. Instead, as PK describes, they are complementary to each other:

> In my opinion, I'd say there is always a connection, there couldn't be none. Every time we work well, it is a form of evangelism. Even though we did not speak about the gospel, people see how we live . . . Challenging people to accept Jesus is actually the last part. Meanwhile, we work in the early phase. As if telling other people that we are Christians, that what we do is a form of worship to God. We tell [people that we are Christians] by the way we work. In my opinion that is a part of evangelism. Isn't it?

Work as Calling

The second theme through which participants describe their vocational stewardship is a perception of work as a calling. This theme is supported through participants' statements regarding the conviction of God's calling for their present work, accompanied by accounts of how they found their calling; accounts of how their calling was reaffirmed through crises; accounts of affirmation of calling at the end of their career; and suggestions offered to new graduates.

Conviction of Calling

A common characteristic observed among participants is a conviction that God has called or led them into a specific work field. At least three quarters of the participants hold this conviction, although the work fields vary. For example, PK says, "What is certain is that when I entered public service, public institutions, those institutions became special. I feel that that's my calling . . . I might change jobs, but I will still remain in the public sector." For some of them this field is also more specifically related to a specific institution, whether an NGO (MI; HC), governmental agency (YI), state company (RT), or private business (RB). This conviction is also embraced by those who formerly worked as professionals but later decided to do unpaid work as homemakers (WO; GT).

Some of these participants remain in one profession, even with the same company or institution from college graduation until the present (BU) or until retirement (RT). On the contrary, others, such as SE, an industrial engineer, and NC, an auditor, simply move from one company to another due to the nature of their field. Many of them, however, have undergone a period exploring multiple work choices before finally committing long-term to a particular field or specific institution (e.g. MI; LT; HC; RB; TB; FG; WI; BX).

Most participants perceive their previous work experiences – sometimes in different fields – as preparation for their present work. For example, LT, reflecting on her upbringing, college experiences, and work experiences before she embarked in her role as an educator in a higher education institution, says, "Yes. I felt that way. Because I can see the red thread [=connecting line] within the process. I mean, God prepared us through skills, abilities, and chances." RB worked for several years as an engineer in a large IT company before he decided to start his own business in collaboration with some of his former colleagues. As an entrepreneur whose company focused on empowering less-educated people to work in IT-related business, RB reflects that his experience working with the less-educated as team members in the previous company was absolutely eye-opening for him regarding their potentiality. He reflects that "God put me at the Assembly [department] [so that] I could meet these kinds of people. At that point I learned to outline telecommunication work to teach them . . . It shaped me. So when I started this business, I just needed to run that."

Finding God's calling
Although elements of the stories that underlie discovering God's calling are usually intertwined with each other, for the purpose of communicative

presentation, detailed accounts will be divided in three different themes of finding calling in one's work: (1) seeing the need; (2) recognizing passion and opportunity; and (3) through supernatural experiences.

Calling through seeing the need

The conviction of calling among participants is related to their detailed accounts of how they found God's calling for their work. Most participants explain that they discovered calling through a natural process such as seeing the need and responding to it. For example, for YI and RT, the need was for more Christian professionals to fight rampant corruption in bureaucracy and state-owned companies. For RB, the need for less-educated workers to be trained and developed became his main focus when he and his friends started to develop their cell tower installation business. For HC it was the need of the poor for decent housing that compelled him to respond with his civil engineering background. For TB, it was the plight of a huge number of Indonesian migrant workers who work in low-paid service work and their need to be empowered through entrepreneurial skills that called him. "I feel that God entrusted them to me. This is something that . . . I tell people, I don't have relatives like them, I don't have the kind of experience like them, but I don't know why I always feel pity for them. [I] Always wanted to help them. That is something that I can't avoid."

Closely related to seeing the need as one of the ways to understand God's calling, HC emphasizes another important element. By looking for a place where a person can make a "value-added" contribution using his/her skills or competencies, one is able to answer that need.

Calling through recognizing passion and opportunity

For some participants, the starting point in discovering their calling was simply passion and interest (WO, TB, MM), or the door of opportunity being opened (BX; BU; DC; CP). But, somewhere along the way they eventually realized that God worked in it. WO found her passion very early in middle school. "So, why do I still stay in this field? I've already loved IT since middle school. I was affirmed by a teacher who said that I was gifted in this field, so I persisted. I was really happy about it. I chose IT too when I went to college." Others, like TB, found it sometime later. "When I was in MBA school, I knew that this is my passion and stopped purchasing engineering books. When I studied civil engineering I didn't know where I was headed. [Later on] I found my passion, I'd say, in business. That's my passion!"

For MM, a hotel manager, the reason she chose to work in the hotel business was simple: "I couldn't work behind a desk." Several years later her work began taking on a deeper level of meaning, only after a major turning point in her spiritual life. Several times she considered quitting her job to join her husband in fulltime church ministry. "But, every time [my husband and I] prayed about it there was no sign to quit. Instead, it seems I was thrown in deeper. So we both agree that God placed me in the marketplace, not in church [work]" (MM). BX, although a law school graduate, initially chose to work in a private trade company rather than pursuing a law career. Her first step in becoming a prosecutor was "just to honor" her friend who provided information about an opening in the Attorney General's Office. "I thought about the opportunity. I will embrace whatever opportunity comes my way. From my life experiences, I realize that God often works beyond my expectations or my hope."

Calling through supernatural experiences

Besides seemingly ordinary ways of finding God's calling, a few participants also experience what appear to be supernatural experiences in the calling to their present work commitment. After playing a central role in reviving a non-profit organization studying public policies, and securing the funding, staff, and president for the organization, MI was trying to find a person to serve as its executive director. At that time, he was working at a factory. To his own surprise, the persons with whom he talked pointed out something that he had never considered. A friend, committed Christian and political activist whom MI believed was a promising candidate to fill the vacant position, declined and said "Why don't you take that position?" The second person with whom he spoke, a well-respected church elder personally unfamiliar with MI, surprised him by responding with a similar question, "Have you considered that you should be the one?" Finally, it was his own brother, who served full time in a different church, who convinced him of God's provision if he walked in his plan. "Then I thought that it was like Psalm 139, whether I wanted to go to the heavens or to the depth of the sea, God was there! The [original] context was to comfort. But [in my case] the context is that I wouldn't be able to run away (laugh)."

For WI, an experience that she understood as God's calling became a turning point to shift abruptly from a promising career in tourism to the totally new field of education. She recalled,

> sometime in 1987 I made a vow to God that if He give me a job that I really love, then He can call me into something He wants afterwards. God did not forget my vow . . . I didn't think about that vow. I have already forgotten . . . but, God really gave me a job that I love. I worked in the service industry, in tourism.

After five years of working in tourism, my perspective changed:

> In 1995 I was climbing my golden stairs . . . then something started bugging me. [It started] maybe around 1996 or 1997. Suddenly . . . I vividly remember what happened. It was an afternoon. I wasn't taking a nap, so it was not a dream. Again, this was not a generalization. This was special. Something happened and only to me. There was a voice, "[the participant's name], you made a promise to Me." I wasn't under a stress, was not discouraged in my work. But I was really surprised. Like Samuel who was called by God, I was reminded. And afterwards I debated with God, like Gideon. I asked for a proof and God gave me the proof [that he really called me to the field of education].

It would be noteworthy that the supernatural experiences that these participants described are related to their decision to embrace the current "secular" works. This explains why it is hard for them not to see that their commitment to the current "secular" professional works is a response to God's calling.

Calling Reaffirmed through Crises

A conviction that God has called participants into a certain work field does not exempt them from crises. Many participants mention that at specific times their journey became so difficult that they were ready to give up. However, it was a reaffirmation of calling, understood as coming from God that explained why they stayed (e.g. YI; RB; RT). Every time she seriously considered leaving her workplace after being mistreated for refusing to cooperate with corrupt practices, YI relates that changes, that encouraged her to stay, happened in her workplace. It was the conviction of God's calling that enabled her to stay until retirement. RB, who developed a private business with the main interest of creating a space for less-educated people, admitted that over a period of eleven years there were times when he considered quitting. Limited human resources for strategic business development in his company, as well as a highly competitive market, brought enormous pressure on him. "Sometimes I felt like I was ready to escape." It was a conviction of his calling that allowed him to remain in his role.

RT testifies that several times he was ready to leave his work at a state-owned enterprise. He cites two examples. "After the first five years I wanted to quit . . . I did well in my work, but the response was not good." He felt his hard work went unappreciated with no incentives and no improvement of professional capacity offered by his employer. "I felt bored. I was ready to leave, either move to a foreign company or go to a theological seminary." At that point he felt God's encouragement to him, "Your work is still in an early stage. It's only the first five years, [it's nothing] if you want to eradicate corruption in Indonesia." He felt God strengthened him to persevere in his mission and "keep going."

Many years later, RT encountered another roadblock after he was assigned as the only local representative to work with international consultants in drafting a white paper for a new electricity law. After three years of work, the law was finally issued. But for reasons he could not accept the Constitutional Court of Indonesia cancelled the law five years later. RT was devastated. He was assigned a second time to draft a renewed law. But he was ready to leave his job. "I thought, I just want to quit . . . I mean, this country does not want to change for the better." With knowledge and experience in electricity law and policy, he thought it would be wiser to begin a new career in another place in which his expertise would be appreciated. At the lowest point, he saw himself like Elijah, the biblical prophet, devastated and full of self-pity after a fierce battle. "Then I was strengthened by God's Word. Like Elijah, the Lord strengthened me by feeding me. 'What are you doing here, Elijah?' . . . Don't stay here! What are you doing here?" It was his conviction of God's calling that enabled him to stay and continue his journey. He finally drafted a renewed electricity law which was successfully issued two years later. He worked in the same state-owned enterprise until his retirement.

Calling Affirmed at End of Career

Several already-retired participants also testify that affirmation to their calling came through the joy and satisfaction they experienced at the end of their career. "When I finished, in my retirement, I felt an inner satisfaction. I said "Lord, I have done my best!"" (RT). Similarly, NQ, at the end of her career as an ophthalmologist, was reassured that "it was my place. I felt comfortable to work in that area . . . I enjoyed working there, even though the stress was high in doing surgery since we were afraid to fail in handling soft tissues." For GT, who chose to become a stay-at-home mom after several years of her professional work in accounting, affirmation came from her children when they became teenagers, appreciating her decision to become a stay-at-home mom, even though later she worked part-time at a publishing house when her children were grown up.

Suggestions for New Graduates

A conviction of God's calling is also reflected in the way participants responded when asked about suggestions for new graduates who are searching for their life calling. Based on their own experiences, most participants confidently suggest several principles on how to find God's calling, considering elements such as the needs of people, "value-added" contributions, interests and passions, and "doors of opportunity" (e.g. CT; LT; HC).

As we shall see in the following section, for most participants in this study, the strong conviction of God's calling in their work is accompanied by a strong sense of purpose to serve others through their work.

Work as Service to Others

The third theme participants describe as part of their vocational stewardship is a strong orientation to work as a service to others. Most of these participants, from various professional backgrounds, view their work as: (1) a service to wider society; or (2) an opportunity to serve the underprivileged. Several others refer to a more immediate impact: (3) upon colleagues and the workplace; (4) to fulfill financial needs of their family; or more general, such as (5) "glorifying God" and "blessing others." A number of these participants refer to more than one of the above categories. But most of those who refer to the first three categories were those who value their work as intrinsically meaningful.

Answering Needs of Society

One third of participants in this study seek to serve society at large through their professional work. They see the importance of a calling to participate in God's work in the public square, such as through their roles in politics (MI; FG), finance (PK; BU), bureaucracy (YI; RT), education (WI), journalism (CP), and housing development (PT).

MI voices convictions regarding the importance of Christian responsibility in the public sector. He views his involvement in politics as serving as salt and light by establishing truth and justice in society:

> How do we prevent decaying in the society? Moral approach, [surely] . . . by practicing honesty, etcetera. But how in terms of policy or in our lives together can we apply that honesty so that honesty is not just a private virtue but a public virtue. We need to learn about this and realize that living together is a part of our responsibility too . . . Do not just prepare yourselves to go to heaven, but also bring that transformation into the society too.

From another perspective, PK, who works at Indonesia's central bank, also asserts similar convictions regarding the strategic role of Christians in public service. Through his role, he believes that he is able to contribute to society with policies and regulations supporting the underprivileged:

> I contribute through policy, through regulations, through orderliness in that part. If we can make good regulations – we have some regulations which end is to make the housing price more affordable; so that poor people have the chance to own a house. The regulations that we made is to ensure such ends. I enjoyed that. That's what we can do.

RT views corruption as something that "God hates," and as one of the primary problems hindering the development of his country. Therefore, serving others by fighting against systemic corruption in his work has become his passion and mission. "After five years [of working], I started to meditate to find ways to eradicate corruption more systemically." Among several initiatives to actualize this mission, one involved developing transparency in the state-owned company where he worked. "Corruption can disappear if there is transparency . . . it's hindered . . . transparency can take the form of a standard operating procedure. Clear standards and guidance. Those were the things that I did. Usually people avoid that. Why? No additional income! Nothing. No credit from their boss." It was a confidence in his calling for this mission that kept him going in the lone journey of battling corruption in his field.

In her calling as an educator, WI is particularly passionate in her training role helping new college graduates prepare for one year teaching in a remote area. She views this as a strategic role to draw future Indonesian leaders into closer relationships with the people. "When they send young teachers to remote areas with the aim of creating leaders who have a grass-roots under-standing, it goes in line with what I see that there are too many leaders with huge gaps with the people who should own this country." Therefore, after investing several years in this movement she reflects,

> The jargon of [this movement] is "teaching for a year, inspir-ing for the whole life." For those of us who are involved [as trainers], it is "teaching for a year, get haunted for your whole life." It's true . . . after a period of time, we have a better un-derstanding of the problems we encounter and become more passionate to fix them!

Other participants share stories from daily life events in order to illustrate their vision and efforts to serve society with their work. For example, when she started her career as a journalist, CP "was hoping that [she] could write inspirational things . . . things that improve people's life quality. [Things that] make people think positively, making a positive impact on people's lives." Even though her intention often becomes a "blur" due to a high workload, she still maintains that vision as her metric. "I use that kind of measure to sort news, to decide which will be worthy to publish." In his work as a banker, BU views his job beyond just providing profits for his company, but also to have a positive social impact through giving loans and accepting savings. "If I give someone a loan it means that someone's business will grow.

If someone's business grows, I'm not just seeing profit for that person, but that he/she can open more job opportunities." Beyond her immediate role as a prosecutor, BX sees her role as a civil servant who must serve people. "There are too many people who don't want to serve others. Civil servants must serve others because they are doing a public service."

Serving the Underprivileged

The second most outstanding work orientation of the participants in this study is a concern and commitment to serve the underprivileged. One third of participants with various professional backgrounds share this orientation. Some of them work in "service professions" such as doctors and educators (NQ; IT; LT), or in NGOs that particularly aim to help the poor (HC; RI). However, it is noteworthy that participants who work as business-persons, politicians, lawyers, and prosecutors (TB; RB; FG; BX) are also among those who have a strong concern for the underprivileged in their vocational journey.

NQ, an ophthalmologist, says one of the reasons she started her own clinic was to help needy people through cross-subsidy. "There are people who can pay and those who cannot. We accept them both." IT, a general practitioner, says, "But my heart is for the needy. I like to serve poor people, people who have no power; I love that. People in [a general hospital] are all like that. They are usually from villages, and I can speak Sundanese, so I can be more involved with them." When she was asked the reason, she replies, "I love to help people like that, to heal them . . . I still maintain a good relationship with many of them. Sometimes they look for me or their grown children will look for me. I love that."

When asked why he chose to work at a non-profit organization providing housing for the poor, HC replied "The vision [of this organization] is a world where everyone can have a livable home. That convinced me that this is the right place for me. To me, its vision fits my vision, and I can apply my knowledge and serve poor people." Another participant whose heart for the least is expressed by working in a non-profit organization is a lawyer. With a strong passion, RI spent the first eight years after completing her law degree working with a non-profit organization to provide legal aid for the poor and legally illiterate people. She finally shifted to another job with more predictable working hours after having a baby and finding it difficult to fulfill both work and family responsibilities while serving with the non-profit.

Besides those whose concern and commitment for the underprivileged is expressed through "service" professions and non-profit organizations, a heart for the least is also strongly evident among participants whose fields are often deemed "selfish" such as those of businessmen and politicians. For example, TB, a seasoned businessman, is passionate about teaching entrepreneurship not only to the educated, but also to the underprivileged and marginalized sectors of society such as migrant workers, ex-prostitutes, and lepers. Regarding migrant workers, he explains that his concern grew since Indonesia actually has a huge number of migrant workers and is ranked third in the world for migrants. "We send out about ten million migrant workers, six million legally," and "from that six million, four million are women." The problem is, as he discovered, that this situation creates dysfunctional families since half of these women have families. "If every mother has two children, there are four million children who are raised only by their fathers, and two million husbands who meet their wives only every two years." He is also concerned that culturally this situation is oppression to women. "There's a village where most women are migrant workers. The women there are considered [true] women if they become migrant worker, be a mother, be a wife, and help the family." As a response to this grim picture, in the past five years he has conducted entrepreneurship training for these migrant workers in several countries where they work. "Since it's difficult for them to come, the trainings can only be conducted on Sundays. It takes about one and half years [for a series]. I can't claim it to be very successful. We have encountered many obstacles in the field." However, these obstacles do not stop him. He says, "I feel that God entrusted them to me. This is something that . . . I tell people, I don't have relatives like them, I don't have the same experiences, but I don't know why I always feel sorry for them. I always want to help them. That's something I can't avoid." His commitment to help these migrant workers even sets the direction of his doctoral study. "My doctoral dissertation aims to seek ways to educate these migrant workers on a wider scale. [So] that when they come back home, they can start businesses in Indonesia, and [thus,] can [be together with] their families."

Another example, RB, an engineer who never had plans to become an entrepreneur, eventually, along with former colleagues, launched a joint venture
business with a strong intention of providing opportunities for less fortunate
people to receive formal education to work in cell tower installations:

> At that time, we discussed that if we wanted to start a business
> we need to have an [added] value. It's not supposed to be just
> profit-seeking. My friends agreed . . . We wanted to make a
> business that trains people. The scope was those below us. The
> target was high school graduates. These people have difficulties
> in seeking jobs. College graduates have better opportunities
> compared to them . . . Let's train, then empower them. My
> friends agreed. Ok, [they said,] we'll train them.

As a parliament member, FG reflects on his role as a representative to underprivileged constituents. "So far I still think that the parliament is a place
to serve. I am given a place to serve. I may not serve like pastors, preaching,
etc. But I serve people in villages, in villages that have no access to the government, or access to the outside world." It is also worth noting that even
BX, a prosecutor, has this perspective of siding with the underprivileged in
her work. She recalls how she finally arrived at that point:

> I thought at the time, why did I become a prosecutor? What
> am I doing prosecuting people? Why am I bringing people
> into prisons? It's hideous. My heart is not like that. We don't
> have anything to do with them. They did not wrong me per-
> sonally, so why do I want to make their life difficult? But then
> my grandma . . . affirmed me. She told me once, "If you want
> to help people, you can do it no matter where or who you
> are!" I then think that God spoke to me through my grandma.
> What she said put me into a deep contemplation [regarding
> my situation]. She's right. In my position, I can help people
> even though his/her status is as a defendant, especially if they
> are the victims of those who reported them. In some instances,
> I can make decisions concerning their lives. In prison, out of
> prison, [and] how long.

Impacting Colleagues and the Workplace

A number of participants also emphasize an intention to impact their workplace and colleagues through their work (e.g. RB; SE; NC). SE, for example, says, "I understand this is also God's work, since I can be a blessing for the workplace community like my boss. He is supported by my high performance, my good attitude with a high standard of ethics, etc. It will surely develop the company." On the other hand, he also speaks about his role with the colleagues below his position.

> When I led one factory, I needed to communicate with the labor union. I led in a way that took their interests into account . . . [by] becoming a boss who encouraged and properly coached them. Thus, they felt comfortable with my leadership and supported me . . . I saw that we actually became a blessing to each other through our work relationships.

NC, an auditor, says, "There were many changes after 6 months working [in that company]. [Initially] no one wanted to stay for very long with us. But when I joined, my prayer was, 'Lord please don't let me not contribute anything to this company.'" She added, "My dream was that the people [in my company] saw us as a strategic business partner. Now they started to see that they need us."

Fulfilling Financial Needs

A few participants also mentioned a valid concern for their family's financial needs as a main purpose for their work, at least during certain life seasons. "My mom was an elementary school teacher. My dad was a junior high school teacher. We were eight siblings, I'm the third. Many of my younger siblings' [education] needed to be funded . . . That was my first mission, it was simple" (SE). For the first several years, WO worked outside home to support her husband in fulfilling their family needs in the first years of their marriage. Afterward, she decided to become a full-time mom at home while still doing volunteer work in her area of expertise.

Blessing Others

Others refer to a core desire "to glorify God" (CP; GT; CT) or "to be a blessing for others" (SE; GT; TO) in their work. For example, CP, a young journalist, says, "Our lives belong to God. Hence, our whole lives are to be dedicated to God." SE, speaks of his big question when he launched full-time into his profession, "That was exactly the question I had in mind when I entered my profession: What is it in this profession that can become a blessing for others?" GT speaks about her double roles at home and in the workplace several years after becoming a full-time mom. Through working in a Christian publishing house, her intention was "to touch people's lives through books." She says, "I learned a lot through books. And I have an intention that books published [from this publishing house] will make people learn . . . and at the end they will encounter God." Of her role at home she shares, "That is our longing, that our children will be used as God's extended hands, through their professions and through other ways . . . The core is that in whatever they do they will glorify God and become a blessing for others."

In summary, the participants' description of their vocational stewardship reveals the three-dimensional shape of vocational stewardship: meaning of work, calling and service. Each dimension contributes to the shape and is interrelated with each other. Vocational stewardship, as they described, is indeed a commitment to serve others and creation through work, based on the conviction of God's calling and valuing both the intrinsic and instrumental meaning of work. This commitment involves multiple dimensions of a vocational stewardship journey: cognitive (conceptual), affective (character), and active (practice). For instance, while their meaning-making of the nature of work occurred mostly in the conceptual sphere, their commitment to follow the path of their calling to serve the underprivileged through their work seems to fall in the affective and active sphere.

The mosaic picture of vocational stewardship from the participants' life stories also helps us to understand more comprehensively of what kind of preparation and support they need to be able to navigate well in their vocational stewardship journey. How did this vocational stewardship develop in these Christian professionals? This is the heart of the question of this study. This will be explored through the findings in the following categories.

Category-2: Development of Vocational Stewardship

The second category of the research findings is phases of the development of vocational stewardship. Based on the participants' responses, there are four phases of vocational stewardship development emerging from life stories that they told: (1) Introductory, in pre-college years; (2) Formative, in college years; (3) Transitional, in the first 5–10 years after college; (4) Generative, in the rest of the years after their transition. This is particularly true for participants with campus ministry background. Most participants without campus ministry background did not follow this pattern, particularly in terms of the timeframe for the formative and transitional phases.

Table 3. Phases of Vocational Stewardship Development

Phases of Vocational Stewardship Development	Introductory	Formative	Transitional	Generative
	Preparational		Actual Journey	
Psychological – Physical	Childhood & Adolescence	Emerging Adulthood – College	Emerging Adulthood – Post-College	Maturing Adulthood
Significance	Cultivating values	Establishing foundations for vocational stewardship	Finding the "sweet spot" & early phase of integrating faith and work life	Integrating – integrated faith and work life

Introductory Phase

Participants in this study refer to their childhood and teenage years as an introductory phase for their vocational stewardship development. Most participants without campus ministry background refer to their pre-college experiences in their family of origin, particularly parental influence and high school years, as significantly influencing the values they hold in their vocational journey. Nevertheless, parental influence and church/parachurch influences in childhood and teenage years are also mentioned by a few participants with campus ministry background, even though their description is less emphatic.

Values

A number of participants refer to their experiences in childhood and teenage years as significantly influencing the values they hold in their vocational journey. The influences that participants experienced vary from the values of integrity, sacrifice, a strong sense of mission, logical and democratic way of living, up to valuing righteousness as a way of living. The influences particularly came from their family of origin (PT; WI; LT; TS; TO) and also from youth groups they joined in church (WI).

For TS, he recalled mostly the role of his former pastor in shaping his values in his early thirties and the role of others in his understanding of the faith and work integration at the age of thirty-five. His recall of earlier influence of values such as integrity and hard work took a leap to the role of his father as a model in his childhood. "His integrity was amazing. He sacrificed extraordinarily for his children. His love for his children was amazing. Praise be to God for he [finally] believed in God and was baptized during his last days." For TO, it was his grandfather, a pastor, who inspired in him a strong sense of mission.

> My grandfather . . . I admired his joy in meeting convicts. He was fearlessly joyful even though he knew he risked to be beaten up. I used to ask, "Aren't you afraid?" He would answer, "No, for I'm not alone. Jesus is with me. When we visit the jail, we bring Jesus's presence with us. Whatever's your ministry, it brings the presence of Jesus!" That inspired me.

Similarly with WI, her parents influenced her with values that she appreciated. They taught her with logic, dialogue and a democratic approach. At home she learned "to see from others' shoes." These habits became very helpful as she pursued her educational calling in the heterogeneous context, culturally and religiously. She says, "That helped me very much when I entered a multicultural world which is so heterogeneous, since I'm used to living with differences." LT, whose parents are both teachers, reflects that she was brought up with an academic environment. To a certain extent that influenced her and prepared her vocational journey as an educator. For PT, his mother's continual prayer and hope for him to become "a righteous person" has always reminded him to be that kind of person in his vocational

journey. In some cases these parental influences continue in participants'
teenage years and even afterward (e.g. NC).

Early Foundation in Teenage Years

Some participants refer to teenage years, especially in high school, as significantly formative for their spiritual life. The influences vary, including the
basics of Christian faith and values, studying the Bible, and ministry skills.
IT, for example, owed her faith and biblical values to her church pastors.
"They were the ones who planted values . . . They planted faith. I think they
were the ones who taught me . . . high school through college years, they
were the ones who planted. I think their role [in this] was very significant."

WI also benefited from her youth counselors within the church that she
joined in her high school years. The multicultural situation in that church
prepared her for deep involvement with similar multicultural situations in
her vocation. She also appreciates the depth of learning that her counselors inspired in her even as a teenager. "We had the William Barclay [New
Testament commentaries] series. So, our Bible Study was very inductive.
When people say about O-I-A [i.e. steps in Inductive Bible Study: observation, interpretation, application] we have learned that in our high school
years." As she told her life stories, she was still impressed with the way she
was being taught by her youth mentor:

> It was even crazier in that golden age that the church allowed us
> to play cards and billiards. There was a billiard table at church.
> But while playing billiards, I was asked, "What was your quiet
> time this morning about?" Another example was when I learned
> how to play Trump Cards and Bridge . . . While playing with
> the cards I was taught: "We eliminate [things] in life. Don't
> we? You have to choose which one is good, which one is right,
> so that you can [succeed in life]." That was while playing cards!

TO recalls that during his high school and college years, it was his pastor
who became his mentor and also a model for him in preparing him with
pastoral skills for his future role as a teacher for high school students. "My
pastor, who was also my mentor, taught me that different situations must
be approached differently. I learned problem-solving hands-on. God used

[my pastor] to equip me . . . [He] also taught me to teach that receiving attention [and care] is a need."

Formative Phase

College years are a significant period for the foundational development of vocational stewardship for most participants with campus ministry background, which comprise about three quarters of the total participants. Common patterns can be identified both in the types of formative experiences and in the factors which contributed to these developments during their college years. On the contrary, among those who did not have campus ministry background, the formative phase tended to be unpatterned, particularly in terms of the time when it took place. For MM, for example, formative changes only started to happen after she experienced a major turning point in her spiritual life, seven years after working in her second workplace. Others mention significant influences in different time settings other than their college years' experience (TS; TG; IT; WI).

The types of foundational developments for vocational stewardship that the research participants experienced in their college years was a mixture of various elements closely connected and overlapping with each other. For the sake of analysis, these elements will be broken down into seven single elements: conversion, biblical framework, values and character, spiritual disciplines, Bible study skills, "soft skills," and work-field exploration.

Conversion

Several participants refer to their college years as a turning point that radically changed their whole life (e.g. PT; WO; YM; CT; MI). For example, PT says "I came to know God because [my mentor] evangelized me. It was clear; the timing turned my life entirely for the better." Similarly, WO reflects on the turning point that happened in college. "I'm thankful. What's clear was that at the time I was converted, my life was immediately changed." In different words, YM articulates the foremost pillar for his further journey of vocational stewardship: "[The] most important pillar in [my] college life was to know Christ. That was the main thing. The most important decision in my life was to accept Jesus when I was in college. It changed a lot of things." As it is obvious from their life stories, this experience served as the very foundation for their whole life journey, including their vocational stewardship journey.

Biblical framework

Several participants refer to their college years as formative years for the biblical framework underpinning their understanding of vocational stewardship, such as calling, mission, and biblical mandates (e.g. CT; LT; RI; RT; DC). For example, LT says that through various learning experiences in her college years, including growth group, doctrinal teaching, seminar, and student conferences, she learned that all kinds of work are "not fragmented" into sacred and secular. "It was all within God's plan. God's calling is for everything. His callings are not exclusive to what looks spiritual."

RT recalls that when he was in college initially he thought that "missionary work is the most noble work," and that mission is limited to "going somewhere [to preach] the gospel." It was his mentor who, as a matter of fact was a foreign missionary, helped him to understand a holistic perspective of biblical mission. DC recalls that some church teaching when he was an undergraduate helped him to understand a fuller picture of both the gospel mandate and the cultural mandate, which serve as a foundation for his understanding of the importance of his future work as a doctor. "Over there, my eyes were opened that we have the gospel mandate and the cultural mandate. My eyes were truly opened regarding the fact that we are here not only to fulfill the gospel mandate. But we also have the cultural mandate responsibility to influence all facets of life."

These biblical foundations are crucial for participants in shaping the meaning and purpose of their professional work. A solid foundation is also important for them to develop further framework to deal with ethical issues in their daily work from a biblical perspective (PJ; MI). For example, MI stresses the importance of developing a biblical framework for dealing with difficult issues in the public arena:

> The political world is just like any other world, but in the political world we often have to make moral, ethical decisions, etc., and we need a reference point for that . . . We need strong biblical principles, so we know which . . . like serenity prayer,

I mean, we could discern which one to . . . which one to say
no, which are grey areas.

Values and Character

Several participants stress the fact that their college years were formative for
the values they hold and the character needed for their vocational stewardship journey (NC; BX; RT; YM; PT; TB; RB). For example, particularly
important values for NC, an auditor, are honesty and integrity. She says,
"From my college days I learned that I have to be honest and have strong
integrity." BX recalls that she wanted to reciprocate after experiencing great
help from a campus ministry community in her college days. Her mentor, who was also the campus ministry leader, told her, "You don't need
to reciprocate [my kindness]. No. Instead, be kind to another person for
me. Let kindness spread like a disease." She says, "I still hold on to that
[counsel]. Similarly, I advised that person [with the same] counsel." For RT,
the perseverance that he learned in his college years was particularly helpful when he dealt with major obstacles in fulfilling his mission in a highly
corrupt work environment. He recalls, "Our growth group learned from
Watchman Nee: Christ's workers must persevere. I remember well learning
how to persevere." It was influential since he and his growth group friends
did not learn it merely to understand it, but to apply it in their daily life.
"The books we learned in growth group, such as *Christ's Worker*, truly shaped
my character, especially to be tough!"

The values formed in college can be both a habit of mind and practice.
In different ways, both can be influential until many years later in the vocational stewardship journey. Sometimes, such as in YM's shared experience,
the values are more related to perspective, though eventually it will influence
practices such as in decision making:

> We're always faced with choices. Sometimes they're very tough.
> I learned to make decisions considering not only the tangible,
> but also the intangible factors. One of [a preacher's] sermons
> influenced me considerably. It was in a [student] conference
> in 1992 or 1993. It was on Isaiah. Before Isaiah continued
> with his ministry, he had to see God's throne in the midst of
> an unstable kingdom. He had to see that behind a seemingly

fruitless ministry, there is a very real yet unseen reality. I try to keep this reality in mind when I decide and act.

In some other cases the values can be embedded in habitual practices. PT, for example, says that the commitment to honesty, which was cultivated in his college years, still affects him many years later:

> I still remember a no-cheating commitment that I made with my friends [in our college days]. While we usually sat at the back of the class, we [decided to] move to the front. That [commitment] lasted through our college years. Even now alarms would blare in my head whenever I'm tempted to engage in actions similar to cheating. It's because I've been disciplined that way. People say actions that are repeated everyday will become habits.

Further, as some participants pointed out, the values became unconscious after years of being influenced or immersed in them. TB, for example, reflects that "the values which were shaped [in my college years] stayed with me. Those values became so ingrained that I unconsciously carry them into the working world." RB gives an example of how the values that he unconsciously brought from his college life can influence his workplace powerfully:

> From my perspective, I wasn't doing anything special. I just wanted to make the environment at work to be more alike to the one at the [student] fellowship. But it made a difference. Once, the technicians commented how we, new engineers, were different from the others. Our relationships were more comfortable and our teamwork was solid. I then realized that what was natural and ordinary at [the campus ministry] was extraordinary everywhere else. To us, [our traditions are] normal. To them, they bring change even though they are simple traditions.

Spiritual Disciplines

Several participants in this study assert that the college years are formative to establish a foundation for their spiritual disciplines such as having quiet times/devotions, praying, and living in faith communities (e.g. PT; HC;

RT; CP). These spiritual disciplines are proven to be very useful later on in their vocational journey. LT recalls that she didn't learn much about the practical aspects of the work life in campus ministry since it was still vague at that point. However, she appreciates the fact the she was "equipped with spiritual disciplines." She says, "These were basics. Ever since [my] college years, we were taught about the importance of prayer, quiet times, having a [faith community], and searching for calling." Similarly, CO says that it was in college, through campus ministry, that she was encouraged to have the disciplines of prayer and quiet times. "Initially it was just a routine. But I think it has been constructive, so that at one point [eventually] I saw it as a need," she adds.

These spiritual disciplines served a crucial role in their journey of vocational stewardship. HC's story is a good example of this:

> We were, of course, taught about spiritual disciplines such as quiet times. For example, when I was deciding whether to choose [a non-profit organization], I struggled with future financial sufficiency. However, when I did my quiet time on the Sermon on the Mount about, "Look at the birds in the sky which I fed!," it spoke to me. The message hit me. The same topic was discussed in a sermon at church. My memory's a bit blurry but I remember the topic was also discussed at a Bible study at [a parachurch group].

He concludes that what has been important for his vocational journey from his college years, "first is growth group, then the spiritual disciplines . . . and then supported by a larger group fellowship." To a certain extent, this thought is shared by other participants.

Bible Study Skills

Several participants also claim the crucial role of Bible study skills for their vocational stewardship journey (RI; DC; MI; PK). The reasons that they explained range from their need to keep their own spirituality, its usefulness to serve others in understanding biblical principles, and its importance to develop their own biblical understanding or judgment in facing increasingly tough questions in their vocational journey. The bottom line is that these skills are crucial in helping them to grow as a mature person who can help themselves and help others in their vocational journey.

Bible study skills are considered to be important for survival in tough situations where normal intake from the faith community is impossible. RI gives a good example for this. "I learned about Bible study from my college years . . . When I went to graduate school, I went to a church-less place . . . I was saved by Bible study. Listening to Sunday sermons on YouTube lacked something."

Beyond survival, DC indicates the usefulness of Bible study skills even further for his vibrant ministry while he was assigned to work as a physician in a remote area which was often considered to be spiritually barren. When he was in college he attended evening Bible classes in his church to learn bibliology and hermeneutics.

> In my opinion, through these materials, the church gave me the hook, instead of the fish. I can do [Bible] expositions by my own. I know how to do it properly. I know how to deliver sermons properly; I know the rules and the methodology. This enriched me to the point that I can do my own Bible study, [and] help others to do Bible study.

The ability to understand the Bible in-depth through independent learning is considered to be crucial in dealing with complex issues in the vocational journey, as it would be hard to keep depending on others to seek biblical counsel on many details (RI; MI; PK). For instance, RI stresses the importance of developing a well-informed biblical perspective in dealing with ethical issues such as LGBT issues and religious freedom when her legal aid organization was involved in advocating these cases. MI stresses the importance of the discipline of regular Bible reading and developing a good biblical understanding as reference points for those who are involved in politics. PK underlines this point when he was asked what was most helpful for him from his college years learning. He says, "Perhaps, the most basic thing was helping me learn how to comprehend spirituality by myself. It helped me grow from a childlike state where I must be guided through every step, asking where I should go or what I should do. Some people depend on their pastor to guide them through every issue in their lives." This self-reliance is particularly important in facing increasing responsibilities and more complex challenges. "We will need to make big decisions in the future and I think I learned a lot [through Bible study]."

"Soft Skills"

The skills that the participants in this study learned in their college years also include "soft skills," such as leadership, public speaking, and program planning. They adopted the skills mostly through training they received and through their involvement in various types of ministry responsibilities (e.g. SE; PK; LT; TB). They realized later that these "soft skills" were useful for their work. For example, LT says,

> I was involved in committees, arranging activities. Now, I'm a professor, guiding [students to do the same things] . . . When I plan a program or consider themes now, my experience in the planning committee [in the student fellowship] comes in handy . . . If I didn't have these experiences during my undergraduate study, I wouldn't be as comfortable doing what I'm doing now.

PJ, who is now in charge of the communication department in his large state-owned institution, recalls the impact of his "transformative" experience in campus ministry related with public speaking skills. "I used to be a very shy person. I dared not speak in front of people – very shy. The first time I spoke in front of people was when I became a worship leader on campus." That experience encouraged him, "More so, when I was given the chance to deliver a sermon on campus. It was an incredible lesson. Now when I speak publicly I have no fear that people will think I'm a fool . . . I no longer have that fear. It happened through a process, and [on this matter] student fellowship was very helpful for me." They are aware that leadership, organization, and socialization skills which they got in campus ministry are common skills that they can get from elsewhere. However, these skills have been useful in their vocational journey.

Work Field Exploration

Outside formative campus ministry experiences, some participants also refer to the significance of volunteering (HC; RI) or freelance work (CP) in their respective fields during their college years. For HC, having two years of volunteering at a non-profit organization that commits to building houses for the poor is an important confirmation to his passion to work for the poor using his academic background in civil engineering. He decided to work with the same organization almost immediately after his graduation. For RI, a year of volunteering at a non-profit organization that provides legal aid for the poor and the legally illiterate people confirmed her passion to work for the legal aid for the poor through this NGO. For CP, it was her freelance experience at her campus press that confirmed her passion for journalism. "Then I worked freelance for my campus magazine. I think I enjoyed meeting people from various backgrounds." This helped her in deciding which area that she wanted to work after graduation.

As has been described, the college years are very important to establish foundations for vocational stewardship, particularly for those who were involved in campus ministry during their college years. Biblical framework, values and character, spiritual disciplines, Bible study skills, soft skills, and work field exploration are among the most important things for vocational stewardship shaped during college years. As will be described later, this formative phase requires a lot of hard work involving the presence of empowering relationships and communities to enable participants to have a solid foundation for their vocational stewardship journey.

Transitional Phase

The first few years after college have been identified by a number of participants as critical years in their vocational stewardship journey. There are at least two major transitions they experienced at this phase: (1) Early phase of integrating faith and work life; (2) Finding the sweet spot in their work life. For those who got married in this period, the additional dimension of marriage life is added into both transitional aspects. They also learned to adjust to their married life, and for some of them, they strive to find the sweet spot between their work life and married life.

There are various opinions on the exact number of these transitional years, such as: three, five, ten, and even fifteen years (RI; RT; SE; GT). More importantly, these participants, based on their experiences and observations, perceive similar phenomenon of the first few years of entering the workplace as a critical time that needs special attention since it could influence people significantly in succeeding in their vocational stewardship journey. Other participants did not as explicitly mention this transition. Their life stories, however, are good examples of, or at least in agreement with, this observation. The first five to ten years after college was a crucial transition time to adjust into a working world, often followed by another transition into a marriage (e.g. WO; CP; LT).

Early Phase of Integrating Faith and Work Life

The process of integrating faith and work life began as soon as one shifted from college to work. For instance, RI, based on her ten years of experience at the workplace, illustrates the struggles of the early phase in integrating faith into the work life: "In the first three years we were so shaken. Entering the alumni world with romanticism and idealism, but then [encountering realities] that was not as good as we imagined!" Although the journey of integrating faith into work life still continued afterward, she differentiates this early with the later phase of her (and others that she observed) vocational journey: "After that the struggle is getting harder, but it seems that we have [developed] a mechanism to pass through it."

Similarly, SE observes that "a critical time for alumni," between six to ten years after graduation, is a crucial transition in integrating faith and work life that will "determine" the rest of their vocational stewardship journey. The reason, he explained, is "because at that time people will think about career etc. This [thought about career] will be much more dominant compared to other things." He insists, "I know it because in that period I experienced confusion. And I saw that happened to my friends as well." Therefore, he concludes, "this period will determine whether after that ten years if alumni will keep on track or bloom in his/her career but ignore his/her other [life] tasks."

Besides adjustments to work life, GT also includes adjustments to married life experienced in these transitional years. She suggests a longer time frame of the age between twenty-five and forty as critical years for various aspects of life. "There are so many life dynamics, up and downs, decisions to make, life choices, difficulties, and such within that age frame."

Finding the Sweet Spot in Work Life

For most participants, the first five to ten years after college was an intense period of exploration to find the sweet spot of their vocation. It was a time to explore choices before they finally landed in a long-term commitment to work in a particular field they believed as God's calling for them. For example, MI, in his search for calling, worked several years as an engineer before he finally found his calling in politics through working full-time in a non-profit organization for the studies of public policies. LT worked two years in a campus ministry organization, went for her master's study, and worked as a counselor in a higher education institution, before she finally decided to stay as a faculty member in another higher education institution. TB worked several years in the civil engineering field before he was finally convinced that business was his passion. "When I was in MBA school, I knew this is my passion, and stopped purchasing engineering books . . . I found my passion, I'd say in business. That's my passion!"

The struggle to find the sweet spot sometimes is not about changing jobs or fields. Instead, what is looked for is an affirmation to stay. For instance, RT, who experienced hard times in bringing his vision to embattle corruption into the daily life of working at a state-owned company, highlights the first few years at the workplace as a critical time to adjust into the "battle-field." His struggle of whether to stay or leave his post after five years of working in that company also illustrates this type of struggle shared by some other participants in these transitional years.

A unique challenge also experienced by women participants who have family is to find the "sweet spot" between their commitment to work life and family life, especially when they have young children (e.g. GT; RI; WO). GT, for example, only after a series of puzzling circumstances that she and her family experienced, and also through affirming messages from her friends, could finally decide to leave her promising career to raise her two toddlers, and only came back to work part-time after they grew up. Similarly, RI also experienced a long struggle to choose between her passion to work at a loved, but time-consuming, legal aid non-profit organization and her baby's need of care and attention. She recalls, "I tried to stay for one and half years . . . [but] eventually I decided to resign, with a lot of tears, because I really loved my work at [this organization]."

Empowering Resources in the Transitional Phase
In this transitional phase, the presence of mentoring relationships and communities are crucial to help them find the sweet spot of their calling, and

for some of them also in their transition into married life. Two examples describe and contrast how this critical phase is experienced with and without the presence of empowering relationships or communities. PK testifies that his first six years of working in a remote area in Indonesia and doing his master's degree in Japan without sufficient support from any empowering relationship or faith community was a desert-like experience. Fortunately, after finishing his graduate studies, he was assigned back to a place where he could have empowering relationships and communities that helped him to thrive. "I can say that in the first six years I was so dry. But what I got [in college years] did not disappear. If I put it into a picture, the graphic in the first part stuck, then after a while it rose up." In contrast to PK's experience, LT experienced good mentoring during her first years in the workplace. The mentoring relationships became invaluable empowering resources in her transitional phase. She reflects that this was a unique phase of preparation as compared to what she received in her college years:

> In college years we didn't talk much about its practical implications. It was vague. But we were equipped with spiritual disciplines, which become basic. Prayer, quiet time, having community, [as well as] searching for calling – that was [continuously sounded] since college years. But what is [calling] like? That was getting clearer once we become alumni . . . Because now we can feel how it is like, what is the connection with me. Having mentors in this period helped me to reflect. "Oh, I see. So, this is how working people do . . . or this should be [my] work attitude."

Generative Phase

Unlike the previous phases, only a few participants referred to a specific type of vocational stewardship development after the transitional years. SE, for example, observed that after the first ten years, alumni are in a different phase in the vocational journey, marked by at least two things: first, they are "able to be stable" in their work and family lives, and second, they are "able to mentor other alumni." However, even without explicit statements, others, particularly who explicitly underline the transitional years in the first few years after college, also implied similar observation with SE (e.g. RI; GT;

RT; PT). RI, for example, expressed her confidence that after the transitional years, alumni will be ready to handle problems more independently. PT also claimed that after ten years in the work life the need for support from a mentor was replaced by a mutual support from his spouse.

The changes, from dependency to inter-dependency, from needing to be mentored to the need of mutual support (accountability partner), from being mentored to become a mentor, and from looking at models to become one of them, seemed to mark the changes from dependency in emerging adulthood in the transitional years, to inter-dependency in later adulthood years, that affect their vocational stewardship journey. These role changes will be presented more fully in the "Empowering Relationships" category. For now, the issue of stability, related to integrating faith and work will be discussed further in this section.

The adulthood years from the age of thirties onwards, named here as the *generative phase,* can be seen as both integrating and integrated faith-and-work phase. Although integrating faith and work is a lifelong journey, some participants, particularly those in their thirties, seem to speak more about their efforts in the process. Others, particularly in their later years of adult-hood, seem to have been able to describe their faith and work as something integrated. Although it would be hard to fully divide the two, for the sake of analysis, the two subdivisions will be presented separately.

Integrating Faith and Work Life

As has been mentioned, the early phase of integrating faith and work is started as soon as one moves from college into work life. While the process of integrating starts in the transitional years, it continues as a lifelong journey. More importantly, there are some fundamental differences of faith and work, and the integration between these two phases. First, in the early part of the transitional phase, the question is mostly whether the faith that they had in college life is possible in their work life (e.g. RI). In the following years of the generative phase the question moves further whether the kingdom vision and values can be fully integrated into their work life (e.g. NC; YM; RB). Second, while the transitional phase is marked by the exploration to find the sweet spot of calling, in the generative phase sometimes they questioned whether they should stay or leave, particularly when they felt frustrated in fulfilling their mission (e.g. YI; RT). The long journey in the generative phase seems to be marked by the challenges to stay faithful and to be fruitful in their calling.

Having described the discrepancies between the two phases, an additional note also needs to be given, which is that it would be hard to draw a strict line between the transitional and generative phases. The fact that different participants come with different observations about the length of the transitional years is one factor indicating the difficulty in drawing a strict line. Some participants also indicated abundant fruition in their transitional years (e.g. DC; NQ), instead of having it only later. This can be another factor. Other than the fact that variation among individuals is wide, the integrating process is also continual. Thus, perhaps a dotted line between the two phases is more representative to the data.

The long years of ongoing strife to fully integrate their faith into their work life is reflected in the participants' accounts of various types of challenges they encountered along the way. The first type of challenge is related to the question of whether they should stay or leave their posts when things seem to be not workable anymore. This could happen at any point of their journey. For example, YI, who worked in bureaucracy, speaks of how she was treated unjustly in her career for her unwillingness to compromise with the corruption practices. At one point she was not given any job for two years. As another example, RB, at certain points when facing hard times in his business employing low-educated people, considered whether he needed to give up his business to just find a job that would be sufficient for himself.

The second type of challenge is related with their work orientation. As they reached success or a privileged position in their career, their intention to serve was seriously challenged. DC, for example, reflects that the biggest temptation for him and his colleagues in their successful careers as doctors was "luxury, comfort, and ease." FG agrees. Serving his "self-interest" became a big temptation for him as a parliament member (who work and live among the elites), while he actually represented voters who lived in an underprivileged area. The spiritual foundations they had in their college years, accompanied by supporting relationships and a faith community, had helped them from drifting away.

Most often, participants spoke about the third type of challenge, which is the corrupted values they encounter in their work environment. Most common is the practice of bribery penetrating all kinds of work and business sector, such as in getting legal permits for housing development projects, getting IT business projects from certain institutions, unofficial fees for journalists, and even pressure for those who work as civil servants not to get involved in it (PT; TS; CP; YI). The challenge is structural and cultural, so that even simply living their biblical ethic of honesty is often considered as an offensive attitude to their colleagues, bosses, or other people. As they gain more important roles in their workplace, more often than not, their decisions also have a larger impact in their workplace and society. Boldness to live the truth, and wisdom to bring its impact into a structural change, is often the challenge of a faith and work integration at this phase (YI; RT; YM). Thus, a solid and comprehensive foundation in the formative phase is a crucial investment for a subsequent long journey of faith and work integration in the generative phase.

Integrated Faith and Work Life

A number of participants, particularly those in their fifties onwards, de-scribed stories that seemed to indicate a more settled conviction of their voca-tional stewardship, and, without necessarily doing it perfectly, more casually putting the concept into practice. For example, from TB's explanation of his passion to teach entrepreneurship to the underprivileged (migrant workers, ex-prostitutes, and lepers), he seemed to be able to move freely between a conviction of calling and putting it into practice, between a strong biblical reflection which was well informed with statistical data and a close partner-ship with both Christian and non-Christian colleagues and institutions, and he was able to embrace both fruitfulness and failures in his attempts. In another example, GT described how in her transitional years she struggled to find the sweet spot between her work and parental role. Years afterward, she seemed to be able to move more freely between both roles, with a deeper reflection on the purpose and meaning of her work in a publishing house, and appreciation of her nurturing role from her grown children.

A different kind of example comes from reflections in their retirement years. A few of them share their satisfaction of walking through their call-ing in their active work years (RT; NQ), and also a commitment to mentor young graduates in their transition to work life (RT; PT). These stories seem to be reflecting a vocational stewardship development that has reached maturity, despite imperfection, in the generative phase.

Category-3: Empowering Relationships

The third category of the findings contains various types of relationships empowering participants for their vocational preparation up to the college years and in their actual journey in their work life. These empowering relationships can be described more specifically by the roles of models, mentors, accountability partners, friends, and also books, in their vocational journey. These roles are not described as strictly separate from one another. Some participants highlight overlaps between the role of mentor and model. Others emphasize that as time went by, their mentors eventually become their accountability partners.

Table 4. Empowering Relationships for Vocational Stewardship Development

Empowering Relationships				
Models	Mentors	Accountability Partners	Friends	Books

Models

One way in which the participants in this study were inspired for their vocational stewardship is through their encounter with models. About two-thirds of the participants pointed to the importance of models in their vocational stewardship journey. These models include historical figures (such as David Livingstone for IT, a medical doctor), as well as contemporary people, whether there is a direct relationship with the participants or not. In some cases, the encounter happened particularly in their childhood (e.g. WI; TO; TS) or through their college years (e.g. PT; RT). However, as some participants refer to role models, they could also be important after college years (e.g. PK; RB).

The Importance of Models

Some participants underline the superiority of having a model compared to merely learning concepts for their vocational stewardship journey (e.g. RB;

MM; PK; CT; CP). Reflecting on his own learning experience with his mentor, RB stresses the point that a living example has a stronger impact than merely studying material:

> Comparing studying material and seeing a model, I think [a] model will have a stronger impact . . . I see [my mentor] as someone who is very inspiring. Often, I was apathetic [in facing challenges at work]. But whenever I came home from a small group meeting, I felt energized. There was no new thought being taught in the small group. We already knew the concepts. But this new energy made us [feel], "Let's do it again, let's fight!" It's not because we didn't know, not because it's a new knowledge!

From another perspective, a few others shared similar convictions (PK; MM; CT). When asked what she would do to help new graduates in their vocational stewardship, MM emphasized that being an example is more effective than merely teaching with words:

> If we patronize them, what is so good about us that we can patronize them? In this case, I agree with [my husband]. We prefer to involve them in our daily lives. And we let them see what we do each day. Just like that. Our daily lives. If we only think in terms of words, it would be useless. Action is more effective. Seeing how we live. They can imitate that.

A model may not necessarily be excellent in all areas. BU, for example, identified different persons who have influenced his life journey in at least three different areas: his mentor in college years for his early spiritual growth, a senior graduate who modelled an ideal worker, and another senior graduate for family life. These models may or may not be from the same professional background. There are general values which they learn from those people (NC, LT). NC, an auditor, says, "I'm not idolizing any auditor. The way I see it, many Christians work in their own field of expertise, and they give something valuable, values that other people can see . . . I'd say that our before mentioned seniors gave an example of how we can learn about faithfulness and consistency. That becomes a model [for me]."

Models in Pre-College Years

In pre-college years, particularly in childhood, participants mostly referred to their parents as their models for certain values impacting them until now in their vocational journey (WI, TO, TS). For example, TS recalled that he learned values such as integrity and hard work from his father in his childhood even though his father was not a Christian at that point. "His integrity was amazing. He sacrificed extraordinarily for his children. His love for his children was amazing!" For TO, it was his grandfather, a pastor, who inspired in him a strong sense of mission.

> My grandfather . . . I admired his joy in meeting convicts. He was fearlessly joyful even though he knew he risked being beaten up. I used to ask, "Aren't you afraid?" [He would answer,] "No, for I'm not alone. Jesus is with me. When we visit the jail, we bring Jesus' presence with us. Whatever's your ministry, it brings Jesus' presence!" That inspired me!

Models in College Years

In college years, these models could be a growth group leader, a pastor who works among students, a full-time worker in campus ministry, or a professional who can integrate his/her faith and work. Encounters with role models positively impacted the participants by inspiring them, which even resulted in transformation. They inspired participants with their spirituality and dedication (MI; PK), a passion for God's work for social justice and human flourishing (YI; RT; RI), and also through their life examples in the professional world (LT; HC). LT, a university professor, provided an example of how an encounter with role models can be inspiring. When asked about her feedback to help Christian students in preparing them for their vocational stewardship, she stressed the importance of providing opportunities for students to meet with practitioners who can serve as role models, and from whom they can learn how to integrate faith into daily work life:

> It's like what I'm doing now in my teaching approach. I invite guest lecturers [for] at least for one or two subjects. There are practitioners such as [a psychologist] whose area is in industry. Thus, the students can ask, "What kind of struggles does this person have? What are the challenges [he/she faces]? What kind

of preparations do I need? What are factors that are considered as helping to survive in such situations?" And since this is related with [faith and work] integration, this person can explain what it's like for Christian values to be at the workplace. We can do this in campus, faculty, or campus ministry [contexts]. I think a good theological foundation is not sufficient if they cannot see its relationship with how they will work in the future.

MI's experience reveals that the impact of an encounter with a model may not simply be inspiring, but may also be transformative. For MI, an encounter with Indonesian professors while living in the US raised a big question of whether he needed to return to serve his home country. This question is especially crucial with his background. "I was born and raised in Jakarta, in a neighborhood which was quite discriminatory against Chinese [-Indonesians] . . . So, since I was young I thought that as a Chinese-Indonesian, it would be better if I got a job and stayed in America because I'm not accepted in Indonesia anyway." A major turning point in his life happened not long after he started his studies at the University of Wisconsin. "When I was in Madison, I joined the Indonesian Christian Fellowship . . . I went there the fall of 1990 and came to know Jesus and joined the [student] fellowship around spring 1991. To me, that was the first step." It was his encounter with Indonesian professors who became role models for him, for their dedication to their home country, that stirred his intention to seek his own calling:

> At Madison, I would visit their homes whenever I missed Indonesian food since there were a number of Indonesian professors [at Madison] that brought the feeling of Indonesia to the ICF gatherings. I came to know the problems that plague Indonesia from the people who discussed them there. I was at first bewildered at the fact that after they pursued such an expensive education [in the US], they were willing to return [to Indonesia] and accept small salaries. Eventually, I came to respect it. I heard the reasons from their own perspectives . . . [They] wanted to return for the greater good, to serve [the motherland]. Those concepts were new to me and exciting too. [I wondered] what shaped their perspective. I mean, isn't it

more important to focus on developing ourselves? Why bother thinking about Indonesia, etc.? That was the starting point of where I started to research more about Indonesia.

Models after College Years

After college years, the impact of models is still important. Their impact includes helping participants learn life values, encouraging them to live according to God's calling, helping them to learn soft skills, "recharging" their spirits, and challenging them to see possibilities beyond what they have achieved in their vocational journey.

Some participants underlined the importance of models in their vocational stewardship journey related with biblical work values embodied in the lives of these models. These lived out values of commitment, integrity, sincerity, dedication, and faithfulness, inspired these participants in their journey (NC; YI; TO; DC). For LT, encounters with people who strove to live according to their calling encouraged her as she was entering her professional life. For HC, models he found at his workplace helped him to learn soft skills such as leadership and management. For RB, an encounter with a model who was also his mentor, constantly recharged his spirit. PK reflected how encounters with certain people stretched his imagination of what he could be, challenged him to see possibilities beyond what he was then:

> Those kinds of admirations helped me and shaped me . . . For now, [those people] who shaped me a lot are people like [a model I knew]. He has weaknesses, but this man is crazy in his commitment to serve God. Those kinds of examples are very clinging, making me often feel ashamed of myself. Then that pushed me to ask myself, "What are you doing?"

Some participants in their late forties to sixties also articulated an interesting reflection that becoming models themselves for younger people has a positive impact on their own vocational stewardship journey (e.g. BU; IT; NC; DC). BU said that when he thought, "'You are a model now!' that meant God gives me a burden to be a model there! To be able to model, we have to maintain and guard our integrity. How can a model get involved in corruption? Or get divorced? That would mess up everything!" Similarly, DC articulated, "For me, one of the boosts was to be a model. We become their model, their shepherd, their role-model. We serve, therefore we have to manage ourselves better because we become the model for them." NC also reflects, "It's hard because I am a senior here. I am seen as a role model. It's hard. Often times, I'm not what you think. I have many weaknesses too. But by that demand we grow!"

Mentors

Other than models, the role of mentors is also considered significant for vocational journey. About two-thirds of the participants referred to the importance of mentors for their vocational stewardship journey. For most participants, this is particularly true in their college years and in the first few years after college. There are a few cases where the role of mentors is also important in pre-college years and after the transitional years at work.

The Importance of Mentors

The importance of the presence of a mentor in a vocational journey was underlined by participants in different ways. MI, for example, argues that for his work field in politics, the presence of a mentor is more important than a model. He argues that, unlike in engineering (his previous work field), there are a lot of grey areas in politics. MI articulated it well in his case that in general, the presence of a mentor is crucial rather than merely having role models:

> In politics, one thing that needs to be prayed for and looked for is a mentor. [Having] a role-model . . . is important. If we pray, we pray for the best, and the best would be a mentor . . . In the engineering world, when you calculate you always get either the right or the wrong answer. In politics, there are many grey areas, vague, all can be compromised. The way I see it, the more we have this kind of work, the more important a mentor is.

From a different perspective, LT also articulates the advantage of having a mentor. For LT, a personal relationship with a mentor, instead of knowing someone merely as a model, allowed her to have accessibility to learn more from the person, including the opportunity to gain insights and feedback from that person in facing tough situations. However, instead of contrasting the two roles, like MI did, LT stresses that a good mentor is also the one who can be a good model. "If possible, our mentor is also a model. So we choose mentors that we see as fitting to be models. I know we human beings are not perfect; we have our weaknesses and limitations. But their efforts, their sincerity in their ups and downs, I think, can become a lesson to learn."

Mentors in Pre-College Years

While most participants referred to the crucial role of mentors in their college years or in the first few years after college, there were a few participants, such as WI and TO, who referred to the significant role of mentors in their teenage years. WI benefited from her youth counselors within the church that she joined in her high school years. She appreciates how her mentors helped her to study the Bible in-depth and learn life principles in her teenage years. TO also appreciates his pastor, who became his mentor and also a model for him during his high school and college years, in preparing him with pastoral skills for his future role as a high school teacher.

Mentors in College Years

The presence of mentors during college years is an important factor causing the college years to be significant in preparing the foundations for the vocational stewardship journey (e.g. PT; YI; PK; CT; BX; TO). Most mentors these participants referred to were their growth group leaders (e.g. PT; PK; CT). A few others referred to full-time campus ministers (RT; BX) or church pastors (TO).

The role of a mentor in these participants' college lives included helping them in their very basic spiritual needs, helping them understanding their callings, and also becoming a role model themselves. For example, PT points to the role of his mentor in helping him to experience a decisive turning point that provided the very foundation for his whole spiritual life journey. Later on, his mentor also helped him as he searched out his calling. "What I remember most was my struggle deciding between the business world and the ministry world. I know that I am where I am now because of the things I learned when I struggled with the decision. During my struggle, [my mentor] said that Indonesia needed its professionals." The advice helped him in the decision-making process to finally pursue his calling as an engineer instead of working full-time in ministry.

PK reflects that his mentor, also his growth group leader in his college years, inspired him as a role model, despite his awareness that his mentor was not perfect:

> [My mentor] isn't perfect. I often criticize him, but he's a patient man and he has us in his heart. I don't know why a General Secretary [of a national campus ministry organization] would give his time to second-year law students. It was amazing to me . . . That was one, and I also know that he studied law like us. He's an amazing role model. A person like him gives his best in coaching us. He shaped me to be the person that I am.

Mentors after College Years

About half of the participants mentioned that the role of mentors was also significant in helping them walk through their vocational journey. For most of them, this was especially true in their transitional years of their work life. There are various ways in which participants described the role of mentors in their vocational journey, including inspiration, encouragement, feedback, affirmation, and support.

A few participants referred to the role of mentor as their source of inspiration in their vocational journey (CT; RT; LT). For CT, whose field is in marine ecology, his mentor, who supervised his undergraduate and graduate thesis, helped him by opening insights about ecology and inspiring him with the love of nature. "He reminded me that the balance of nature is created by God and we need to maintain that. Although he did not say that this is a cultural mandate, that one is the gospel mandate. He sees it from a scientific perspective. He was the one who planted in me the love of nature." In a different context, RT appreciated his mentor who inspired him with the passion to fulfill God's mission by dedicating his life for the nation:

> He encouraged me to do something for this nation. He's the person that is significant in my life because he set my inner life on fire every time I see the map of Indonesia, I was burned. He did that. His words, God's anointing made him that way. "Look at that!" Until now, whenever I see the map of Indonesia, there's always a thrill. Because he always [encouraged me], "Let's do the mission!"

Another role of a mentor that participants referred to is encouragement, particularly as they faced hard times in identifying and working through their callings (RT; CT; MM; TO). The person who inspired RT to serve his nation through his professional life was also the same person who encouraged him to stay faithful at crucial times when he was so discouraged he was ready to leave. "No turning back! That's what God wants to do through us. I know you are struggling. But that's the mission God wants to do through you!" Encouragement to stay faithful in his calling was also what CT experienced from his mentor at the lowest point when he was ready to give up. After several years of waiting and being treated unfairly for his application to be a faculty member in the same campus where he did his college and master's degree, he decided to look for other possibilities. One of them was a government-funded research institution:

> And then I was summoned [by a research institution]. There was a letter of summons. It happened that I lived at my professor's house when it came. He was my sponsor. He received that letter. And he asked me, "So, do you want to be a professor or a researcher?" I answered, "Sir, what do you think? You see how I have always been blocked [from being a professor in this campus]. Perhaps God doesn't want me to stay in [this campus]." He only said, "Just be patient!"

It was a short, but timely and meaningful, conversation with his mentor that helped him to make the right decision at the crossroad of his vocational journey.

Another kind of encouragement was experienced by MM, a hotel manager, when she faced difficult times dealing with her bosses. At one point, her boss brought his syncretic beliefs to be practiced daily by employees. "When I told [my husband] about my experience, 'Why is my GM so weird?' He would encourage me with, 'That means you have climbed up a rank. You used to only deal with emotions. Now you deal with something that is not of our world.'" For TO, his mentor was the one who could see his potential – the mentor equipped him and encouraged him to fulfill his mission as a religious teacher in a public high school.

For MI, who works in politics, feedback from a mentor was crucial in navigating through a lot of "grey areas" in his field. Similarly, LT also saw the important role of a mentor inspiring like a model and providing valuable feedback. She stressed further that what younger alumni need is someone who can give them feedback in sharpening ideas, instead of someone who tells them what to do. "I think alumni are not that passive. They have their own thoughts, but need others to discuss them. Brainstorming. 'Is my idea wild or what?' Not somebody who says, 'You have to do this or that!' No. They have their own thoughts!" With their feedback, LT added, mentors could affirm and enrich young alumni's thoughts. "Because they have been there longer, our minds can be opened for things that we did not consider. So our consideration can be more mature." In a slightly different perspective for WH, the role of mentor is like a mirror for her. "Mirror . . . literally a mirror! All of my life experience, I shared it with others, to my spiritual mentor. That might be it. For me, their presence is a God-given mirror."

Support is another role of a mentor that participants referred to (BX; WI; GT). When asked how her mentor helped her at times when she was facing tough challenges, BX, a prosecutor, replied, "Sharing and praying. Every time I saw [my mentor], I always said, '[. . .], please pray for me. My work is like this.' She'd answer, 'Of course. We all pray for you. Not only you, but everyone in the field of law.' It is a great challenge for this field in Indonesia. We are facing a very serious problem in this field of law." In a different context, which was the transition in her family life, GT experienced support from a senior couple. They were like "spiritual parents" to her. "They were very attentive. Like when I was confused, puzzled, they always reminded me of what God really wants to do in our lives. What is the most urgent? What is the most important? What are we to do?"

Accountability Partners

Some participants referred to the important role of accountability partners for vocational stewardship. Since a significant number of participants referred to their involvement in growth groups/small groups as something significant for the preparation of their vocational journey in their college years and also in their actual vocational journey (this will be presented in the fourth category, Empowering Communities), the role of other small group members as accountability partners is also assumed (e.g. explicitly mentioned by RT and GT). Their roles will be described in the growth group/small group section. However, some participants also specifically referred to the important role of accountability partners outside the small group context (FG), or the shift from a mentoring relationship to a more mutual relationship that they experienced with their former mentors (MI; SE).

The Role of Accountability Partners after College Years

The role of accountability partners after college years is not too far from the role of mentors, such as to help the participants keep on track, experience mutual encouragement, and get constant feedback, but in a more mutual relationship. For FG, for example, the emergence of someone who committed to minister him as an accountability partner has been very helpful and allowed him to do reflection regularly and to receive feedback in facing various challenges as a parliament member:

> After the first year [in parliament], we did a reflection. "You have a chance to be a parliament member. That's a journey. Let's reflect on the journey." Well, I was reminded that I am here not because of money, not because of my own strength, not because I was close to people of power . . . Just reflection. Then we talk about why I am placed in the parliament? I felt that by doing that weekly I was strengthened. Or if I started to go astray by following other people's ways of thinking, I was reminded again.

In some cases, participants met an accountability partner whom they did not know beforehand but who eventually played a significant role in their vocational journeys (FG). In some other cases, mentoring relationships that may have started in college years or afterward, shifted toward more of a mutual partnership as time went by (SE; MI).

From a Mentor to an Accountability Partner

Mentoring relationships are not static. As time goes by, the mentored person matures and situations change. A more directive role of mentor then naturally shifts to become more mutual as accountability/discussion partners. For SE, the mentoring relationship started in college and continued when he entered work life. The mentoring relationship prevailed in the first few years after college, and later on it was more like a mutual partnership. "Now we are more like partners. I give a lot of input and I also learn," SE describes.

To a certain extent the need for an accountability partner instead of a mentor, or the shift from a mentoring relationship to a mutual partnership, is related to age and maturity. For example, PT argued that a mentoring relationship mostly fit up to the first ten years after college, but afterward the need changed to more mutual support. "When our levels differ so much with the new [graduates], half-advising might still be acceptable. But when ten years have passed, we would be more like friends." He suggests that a growth group setting where no one acts as a teacher would fit the need for mutual support in the later years of a vocational journey.

MI gave another example of a shifting relationship from mentor to a more mutual partner. He reflected on his own experience of his mentor in the college student fellowship group who used to influence him a lot – "mostly in spiritual growth." He said, "Now we are more co-workers and maybe accountability partners who help each other to keep on track. When I am discouraged, he can help encourage me. And as a friend we can share that the vision that we talked about in ICF, we are walking it now." He underlined that "these roles change because people also change. I'm changing too. And conditions change!"

The Dynamic between Mentoring and Mutual Relationship

However, the role shift may not be clear cut. Mentoring relationships and mutual partnerships could be blended in a dynamic relationship. As in SE's experience, although there was a major shift from the mentoring relationship in his college years to the mutual relationship in the later years of his work life, there was interplay between the two types of the empowering relationship that he experienced. He recalled, "I saw his role sometimes as a partner, sometimes still as a mentor. At one time he became a discussion partner for this and that. At other time, he would admonish and remind me. And conversely, sometimes I could also give him feedback. The pattern depends on the situation at hand."

Similarly, MI also argued that the shift may not be necessarily from exclusive mentoring to exclusive mutual partnership – "like binary one and zero." Instead, it is more like a dynamic shift in "proportion" between the mentoring and mutual relationship. He argues, "I suspect that actually the [mentoring] relationship naturally enters other phases too. If I'm close to a mentor, over time I will be more comfortable with him/her . . . Maybe the mentoring becomes more balanced with the accountability, so we can talk more comfortably." He explains the reason:

> A good mentor will respect us as equal beings. He will not always see us as his inferior. So, over time, he will eventually treat us . . . I mean, [like my work relationship with my boss], basically more and more decisions are relinquished to me. Sometimes he'd ask me, "How about this?" For me, if we are talking strictly about a mentor, you're not going to ask me that question. But he then respects me and wants my point of view as well. The way I see it, mentor and accountability partners are sometimes difficult to distinguish. A good mentor knows when to adjust himself, probably.

Friends

Some participants also described a diverse support network that has been significant in their vocational stewardship journey, but could not fit into the existing categories of model, mentor, or accountability partner (MI; WO; YM; WI; GT). Similar to accountability partners, but with a looser relationship, they can be categorized as a network of supporting friendships.

Friends may contribute to the participants' vocational journey through their insights, affirmation, support, and challenges. LT, for example, referred to an insightful comment from one of her senior friends that led her to choose educational psychology instead of clinical psychology for her graduate study. She also referred to a conversation with another friend who contributed something at work that affirmed her in choosing a job in a new educational institution, with more challenges but also opportunities for more significant contributions, instead of working in a more established institution.

Besides mentioning mutual support that she enjoyed with her friends, GT also described the significant role that her friends played at the major crossroad where she needed to choose between her role as a mom for two preschool boys and her career opportunities which would also meet financial needs alongside of her husband's income. In that critical situation, all of a sudden, an older friend whom she respected sent her a letter containing a poem. The title was "Children Won't Wait." She recalls,

In the poem, it was said that I will be like "god" for the children, from the time they are babies to their teenage years. They will not wait for you. They will not wait until you have some spare time for them. But they will keep growing, and you will lose chances to raise them, not to mention bringing them to know God and becoming God's children.

The poem made her sleepless the night after she read it. At almost the same time some other friends from her previous workplace, who lived in a different city, also sent her a letter. She recalls, "There were several names on a piece of paper. All of them reminded me of what I was thinking, 'What are you looking for?'" When GT was asked why they sent her that letter, she replied, "I don't know. I was astonished. There was no social media at the time, no phone at that house, no cell phones. But, well, I was astonished. I don't know why, but they still pray for me." The two letters from her friends played their part in helping GT make her decision at one of the major crossroads in her life's journey.

Books

The significance of books was among the things mentioned by some participants (WO, IT, MI). Like models, even though books have only a one-way relationship from the authors to their readers, their influence can be significant. Their influence is also not limited by participants' age. For WO, due to her busy activities in her college years, the role of books was important for her spiritual growth. "I grew [spiritually] mostly through reading books. Sometimes when I struggled with issues, I would get a book and read it . . . I couldn't participate in many campus ministry activities because I worked. Where else would I learn? From Christian books!" For IT, books led her to a meaningful encounter with a historical legend, David Livingstone, who became her role model of a medical doctor with a fully dedicated life to serve.

Books also inspired MI in his role as a Chinese Christian in Indonesia. He recalled an author who wrote about Christianity and the nationalistic movement in Indonesia. "He studied the history of how Christianity in Indonesia met the nationalistic movement and how C. L. Van Doorn, the Dutch missionary, helped Johannes Leimena and the nationalistic movement of GMKI. I learned that Christians had a contribution in Indonesia['s independence].” Other than that, he also read the biography of Yap Thiam Hien, “a Chinese-Indonesian, who loved Indonesia and was widely respected.” Those books were not only inspiring but also life-changing for him. He recalled, “Those readings, in addition to meeting Indonesian professors who were foreign educated yet willing to do something for Indonesia, piqued my interest. Not necessarily interested in stepping into politics, but simply to see that as a Christian and an Indonesian, God must have a plan for me!”

The Diverse and Dynamic Nature of Empowering Relationships

A Diverse Network of Empowering Relationships

The network of empowering relationships (models, mentors, accountability partners, and friends) could be embedded in different communities (workplace, church/parachurch, small group). GT, for example, described four significant supporting networks that contributed to her vocational journey, including her work life and married life:

> There are those from [a campus ministry fellowship group].
> There are friends from church. There are friends from [my
> previous workplace] and friends from [my later workplace]
> who keep in touch by meeting, chatting, doing Whatsapp and
> praying with me for each other. Supporting [each other]. Those
> are friends who support us in our life journey. They came from
> several groups: small group, workplace, church friends, and
> other friends from outside those groups.

Another example, WI, an educator, described a number of people whom she believes to be significant as her supporting network. Some of them became like her mentors in different time periods. Some others are friends who have similar passion in education. With her involvement in a religiously plural organization that sends new graduates to teach in remote areas for a year, her supporting network also includes non-Christian friends.

Non-Christians Models and Mentors

While most examples of models and mentors that participants mentioned are Christians, there are also non-Christians models and mentors that they referred to. Sometimes their role can be very significant. For example, throughout more than two decades of working together in an increasingly developing courier company, TG learned more about generosity from the way his Muslim boss set the company policy in favor toward those who are needy:

> His practice is always setting apart a budget for . . . many things, he really has social concerns. He is always suggesting to us that we involve orphans, widows, the blind in our activities . . . We see [him] as a model. He gives alms indiscriminatingly, to anyone. Sometimes we wondered; we were puzzled. He gives his money to everyone. Actually, I was someone who was full of calculations. But after following [him] and seeing how he gave without calculations as a norm, I now follow him.

In regards to mentors, while some mentors are seen as spiritual parents, there are also non-Christian mentors whose role is important in certain aspects of the participants' vocational journey. For RI, for example, it was her boss in her early career in the legal aid organization. "He is not a Christian. He is a moderate Muslim whose perspective is very good to me. He doesn't judge my faith, but he often invites me to think. 'Try to think deeper [about these issues].' He was the director of [the NGO where I worked] at the time." For CT, it was his non-Christian professor when he did his doctorate in Japan who became his model. "He reminded me again that there are so many things, natural phenomena that we do not know. Although he did not say that natural phenomena reflect God's glory, but he says, 'We need to explore this, so that we can guard this nature.'"

Living in a culturally and religiously diverse world, the contribution of non-Christian friends, models, and mentors, not to mention book authors, are often intertwined with the contributions of Christians as part of the empowering relationship network for the vocational stewardship journey.

The Dynamic Nature of Empowering Relationships

The dynamic nature of all kinds of relationships within this network of models, mentors, accountability partners, and friendships that support the participants in their vocational stewardships is indicated in the ways in which these relationships appear or disappear, increase or decrease, and influence in different periods of time (MI; WI; WO). To a certain extent, MI's description sums up this phenomenon well:

> There are people who at certain times have big influence, but maybe only at the time. Afterwards, not that they are not influential, just simply in my life journey afterwards they do not influence me that much. So, what I found out was that not everybody has continual influence all the time. Probably only now, they at some point in time, made an influence. Some people only make a one-time influence. For example, there was a friend who influenced me a lot and made me actively involved in student fellowship. However, we lost contact for a long time until now. Meanwhile, there is someone like [my current boss], because he's still the president [of this non-profit organization] and I'm close to him. He's like a mentor to me, and has nurtured me a lot about these things. [My previous mentor], who after returning [to Indonesia] did not have a lot of contact with me, just once in a while, in a small group activity, etcetera. But then when he found out [about this organization], I asked him to join and help in [this organization]. He's becoming more of an influence once again.

It is worth noting that the college years have also been important to participants in this study in developing networks of empowering relationships crucial in their lifelong vocational stewardship journeys. These networks developed in various ways. For some, a growth group provided long-term friendships for mutual support in the vocational journey (e.g. SE; GT). Others benefited from the broader campus ministry network, in the same or different cities, to find mentors, models, and new growth groups after their college years (e.g. LT; RT; RB; RI), or a mission-minded faith community of Christian professionals for mutual support in their vocational stewardship journey (e.g. YI; IT; NQ). For IT and WI, they followed their church pastors in their high school years, but also benefited from the campus ministry alumni network and found mentors and mutual support in their vocational stewardship journey.

The role of a network of empowering relationships which includes models, mentors, accountability partners, friends, and also books, in vocational stewardship preparation and journey have been presented in this section. These relationships are embedded in various types of communities. However, since the roles of these communities in vocational stewardship preparation and journey are beyond merely facilitating these relationships, they will be presented in the next section as a separate category.

Category-4: Empowering Communities

The fourth and final category of the findings contains various types of community that empower participants in their vocational preparation and in their actual journey. The empowering communities mentioned can be described as three basic types: family, faith based, and non-faith based. The faith community, which is most often referred to as an empowering community, will be divided further into various sub-types: specific age/stage faith communities (youth ministry, campus ministry, and workplace ministry), growth group/small group, and local church. Active service across various faith communities will be described in a separate section because there are a significant number of participants that referred to its importance in integrating their faith into their vocational stewardship journey.

Table 5. Empowering Communities for Vocational Stewardship Development

Empowering Communities				
Family	Faith Community			Non-Faith Based
of Origin (Parents) Formed (Spouse)	Campus Ministry/ Workplace Ministry	Small Group	Local Church	Workplace Community, Professional Society
	Active Service in Faith Community			

Family

Family is one of the most basic empowering communities in which the seeds of values for the vocational stewardship journey can be sown from an early age where influence often continues throughout the journey. About two thirds of the participants referred extensively or briefly to the importance of their family in their vocational journey. Several participants referred to the role of family in their introductory phase, in pre-college years. There were very few references to familial influence during college years or in the first few years after college. However, the strong role of family influence reintegrates in the generative phase, particularly through spouses.

Family of Origin

Several participants referred to the influence of their parents and/or grand-parents for values such as integrity, dedication, a sense of mission, and valuing others – which they themselves now also hold in their own vocational journey (TS; TO; WI; LT; PT). They learned these values mostly through what they saw, heard, and experienced in their daily family life. For example, TS learned the value of endurance, integrity, and sacrifice, from the way his sightless father kept working hard and lived a very simple life to provide for his family. WI recalls some experiences where she learned how logical conversation and dialogical decision making were made in her home. LT reflects that she was brought up in an academic environment because both her parents were teachers. To a certain extent that influence has prepared her for a vocational journey toward being an educator. For PT, his mother's continual prayer and hope for him to become "a righteous person" continues to remind him to be that kind of person as he pursues his vocational journey.

The role of the family of origin as an empowering community may extend through adult years and also through extended family members. A number of participants also mention their parents, siblings, or in-laws as significant supporters who shared their advice, encouragement, or inspiring life and prayer (PT; NC; LT; TG; GT; BX). For example, NC was under strong pressure from different sources when her financial audit findings indicated a serious violation of certain guidelines in an institution that received funding from the World Health Organization. It resulted in the dismissal of one officer and the postponement of her audit submission for eight months. When asked what was helpful for her in that situation, this is what she replied:

> I'm thankful that I have a mom who loves God. My mom is a full-time Christian worker. She told me, "If you know that it is the right thing to do, don't be afraid, God will help you!" She reminded me that our help comes from the Lord. The Lord is

my refuge. The Lord is my rock. That assured me at the time, and I did not waver to increase or polish the performance [of the organization that I was auditing]. For example, correcting their reports to push funds.

Spouse

The crucial role of a spouse in the journey of vocational stewardship was mentioned by about half of the participants in this study. Although their roles overlap with the previous role categories of model, mentor, or accountability partner, it is noteworthy to devote a separate section on the roles of a husband or wife in a vocational stewardship journey. The roles of spouse, whether as model, mentor, or accountability partner, depend on each participant and his/her spouse situation and background. However, as participants entered marriage, which for most of them occurred in the second half of their transitional years after college, the role of spouse started to become important for their vocational journey. Their roles became even more important in the later years of adulthood as they appreciated more mutual support instead of hierarchical support such as mentoring. "When I was 35, I thought 'why do I still look for a mentor? The Bible said you should have been a leader.' Other people's experience endorses that. So from then on, I didn't have a special mentor, just my family [=spouse]" (OS).

For MM, her husband became a model and mentor in her vocational journey in a hotel business. They worked for quite a number of years at the same workplace before he left for a ful- time pastoral ministry. She recalls,

> I'm thankful that in the year 2000 I was converted, and in 2002 I got married to him. He is somebody who can be a priest at home which brought me to think that whatever we do has to involve God and finding out whether this is what God really wants. I was nurtured mostly from our sharing and also from listening to a local Christian radio station every day.

For SE, his spouse, who has a strong spiritual foundation and similar work background, has become his dialogue partner for issues he faces in his vocational journey. He described their partnership:

She was nurtured by [a parachurch ministry organization].
She is very strict in principles. So sometimes she criticizes me
when my mind wanders, or something else. She's my guardian.
Sometimes she's pretty loud. But I take it that she's right. So
sometimes, in those situations, I feel guarded by her. Guarded
in the sense that she's my partner that gives me input that
sometimes does not occur in my mind. Giving me advice [and]
becoming my discussion partner. It has been quite helpful because she has a strong background in small group. She can give
me insights that complement my traits, complementing my
knowledge. We often discuss. If we have the same problem, for
example, we discuss it. She works in more or less similar industry as mine. We often face quite similar situations. Principles
that we can apply in the workplace, what kind of attitude we
need to build, how we interact, etcetera, are all connected.

For RT, his wife has been a stay-at-home mom and is a consistent prayer
partner and encourager. Although his wife was not directly involved in his
work, throughout his active years in his vocational journey, her support
was crucial:

Imagine, for thirty years, every day . . . We didn't know what
we know now as family altar. Because my wife was a [full-time
worker in ministry], it was common for us to pray [together].
We pray for this nation and this country every day! Every day!
Not just passing time. No! We pray for the president, cases,
events, conferences, or anything in [the parachurch ministry
where we involved]. My wife is well-informed, and we pray
for those, every day. And I believe community in the family
gives an inner strength. No one can see it. My wife is not high-
profile. But she is strong for me, supporting me – never bugged
me for materialism. No. She's very simple. She often encourages
me when I'm weak . . . So, beside the church, my family is the
one who can make me go out of the house upbeat.

Faith Community

For two thirds of the participants in this study, the faith community has been most significant and helpful in their vocational stewardship preparation in college years and in the actual journey afterward. Most participants perceive community as a continuing need, not only during their college years, but also in their work life. Some related this with the need of support in the "critical" first years of transition into the work life (e.g. SE; GT). Many others see a faith community as a continuing need regardless of the time (e.g. YI; PK; BU). As BU says, "In my experience of working and living in different cities, it's definitely positive . . . If I am not involved in a community, it can weaken my vision in work . . . Community helps us to share, to be reminded, to share the burden with them, to listen to what our friends have to say."

The Importance of a Faith Community

In what ways is a faith community considered crucial for the actual vocational stewardship journey? There are various answers to this question, including helping them to keep them "on track," to keep "the flame," to find mutual encouragement, and to connect with "resources." Some participants speak about the importance of the faith community in keeping their vision, or in other words to keep them on track in their calling in the midst of routine work or in facing tough challenges (RB; BU; CT; NC; CP). CP articulates this point by saying her vision is "easily distracted" with "fatigue, routines, [intense] work rhythm, [and negative] responses." She claims that the community, including her spouse, family, and those who work in similar professions, keeps her on track. Recognizing the difficulty for individuals to stand alone, RB also emphasizes the need for the faith community to help Christians stay on track in their calling:

> At least when we are about to get out of track, there are people who would remind us: "Be careful!" Even when we are already out of track, these people would draw us back: "Come on, come back!" . . . Actually, if we have a good relationship with God we should not be easily strayed. But in reality, our work routines and everything makes us stray. That's where fellowship in community comes in handy."

Other than the limitation of an individual, LT stresses the limitation of the non-Christian community as a supporting community in a vocational journey. The faith community helps her to see things at work with biblical values, beyond universal values.

Several participants mentioned the importance of the faith community for mutual encouragement in their vocational journey (PK; SE; DC; CT; GT; BU). For PK, the faith community made a significant difference in whether his spiritual life flourished. Thus, he asserts the importance of the faith community to "keep the flame." He says, "Actually it is as simple as keeping the fire burning. In [a remote area in Indonesia], although I said that my experience was 'dry,' it taught me many things. Especially that afterwards I see that we better strive to stay in a community that could sustain each other's fire." From another perspective, SE claims that the workplace fellowship in his office, where he was its leader for five years, helped its members to remind each other to live with biblical values at work and also to encourage each other to do better in their work.

Another important role of the faith community in the vocational stewardship journey is to enable people to connect with resources. A number of participants refer to the importance of the faith community as a place where they found models, mentors, accountability partners, friends who share the same vision, and valuable information such as good books (WO; DC; TO; SE; TB). Some participants also point to the role of different types of faith communities as a mentoring community in their life transition into the work life and family life. WO offers a good example:

> I was nurtured a lot by [a parachurch ministry serving families] as well as [a campus ministry organization]. They were like interwoven somehow . . . [The parachurch ministry serving families] helped us at the time as young couples to be better couples. I learned my role as a wife and as a teacher for my children . . . [The campus ministry organization] helped me learn more about student life [as well as] professional life.

The forms of faith communities that participants referred to vary, including specific age/stage faith communities like youth ministries, campus ministries, workplace/professional ministries, growth groups/small groups, and local churches. Due to its significance referred to by participants, active service across various faith communities will also be described in a separate section.

Specific Age/Stage Faith Communities

While there were a number of participants referring to the role of their parents in sowing the seeds of significant values for their vocational journey, none of them referred to the role of the faith community in their early pre-college years. The role of the faith community for their vocational stewardship preparation, in terms of the foundations of their spirituality, started to appear in their life stories as early as in their high school years through church youth groups or other kinds of church life (e.g. WI; IT; TO), even though at least half of them came from Christian family backgrounds in their early childhood. However, references to specific age/stage faith communities appeared very significantly during the participants' college years and afterward. Therefore, these two will be presented in the following sections.

Campus ministry

For most participants with campus ministry backgrounds, comprising three quarters of the total participants in this study, formative experiences during college years were mostly embedded in their campus ministry experiences. To a certain extent, RB's assertion reflects their transformative experiences in campus ministry: "For me, my experience in campus ministry was very influential because I went through many life-changing experiences there." The campus ministry was the faith community through which they encountered models and mentors, experienced growth groups, received biblical teaching they need, and were shaped in their values, character, and skills through ministry responsibilities and the overall community lives.

For most participants with campus ministry backgrounds, various types of fellowship group meetings within and outside their campus contributed to the foundational biblical teaching they needed for their basic spirituality and vocational stewardship. CT, for example, says that through many large group meetings that he attended he "was helped to understand calling, gospel mandate, and cultural mandate." RI recalls that the student conferences and retreats she attended addressed the nation's situation. She also remembered that there was a series of Bible studies on the book of Amos for the student leaders in her city. It affirmed her concern for social justice and framed her biblical understanding on the issue. A number of participants also referred to student conferences they attended, especially the national student conferences with their emphasis on holistic mission, as a significant milestone in the preparation of their vocational stewardship journey (e.g. HC; YM; LT; RI).

Within the context of campus ministry, they also learned biblical foundations for their spirituality and vocational stewardship through small groups. Since this influence was often mentioned by participants (by at least half of them), and also occurred after their college years, participants' references to growth groups/small groups will be presented in a separate section. Values, character, spiritual disciplines, and "soft skills," are among other things learned by participants through their involvement in various kinds of campus ministry group dynamics as a community: large group and small group meetings, formal and non-formal interactions, also active and passive participation. Active involvement through ministry responsibilities is an example of formation through active participations, which significantly influenced their character and skills for their vocational stewardship journey (e.g. PK; TB; SE; LT).

Workplace ministry

There are at least two basic types of workplace ministries that participants referred to: (1) Workplace fellowships. It usually has regular meetings (such as weekly large group meeting), and other activities organized by and for those who work at the same office or workplace (PT; SE; HC; DC); and (2) Graduate fellowships/professional groups. They usually have meetings (with varied frequency like monthly or more frequent), and other activities such as retreats and conferences, organized by and mostly attended by those who have campus ministry background (IT, YI).

The importance of each type is referred to by these participants. For example, SE speaks about the significance of the workplace fellowship in his experience: "One of the things is that I had an office fellowship group . . . The content [of its meetings] was really encouraging to us to have better attitudes compared to [others]. I was the fellowship leader for five years." DC claims that the workplace fellowship in the hospital where he worked had at least three benefits for the medical and paramedical workers in that hospital: first, easy to reach for a fellowship meeting in the midst of their busy work activities; second, it developed connections among the workers;

and third, the biblical message being preached or learned was more effective, such as with highly "relevant illustrations" since the audience shared the same context. On the other hand, YI stressed the importance of the graduate fellowship group which she joined for a number of years. "Well, even though I don't have a small group, I have a [larger] fellowship group. That's why I'd say that even though small groups are important, such community is very important to me!" The weekly meeting and bi-annual retreat with similar groups based in two other neighboring cities become a significant supporting community for YI, IT and others for many years.

Looking at the importance of the faith community in vocational stewardship, some participants stressed the importance of ministry to professionals (IT; RT). To underline the significance further, IT compared and contrasted the length of time that people spent in work life compared to college life. "School only lasts for seven years. We do our profession for thirty years. So, we need more ministry groups in professions!" (IT).

Growth Group/Small Group

The significance of growth groups/small groups as an empowering community in the preparation for and actual vocational stewardship journey was referred to by a significant number of participants in this study. More than half of the participants noted its significance in their college years, and more than one third of the participants also mentioned its importance in their work life.

Growth group/small group in college years

Growth groups/small groups in college were referred to by more than half of the participants as the most influential or one of the most influential formative factors that laid the foundation for their vocational stewardship journey (e.g. PT; PK; BU; HC; TB; RT; CT; GT). Perhaps HC's claim represents all their voices regarding the value of small groups in the college years: "Hence, in my opinion, growth group holds the most importance among other activities. Larger group meetings were generally edifying, but growth group was very helpful [for me]." Typically, growth group refers to a small group with several members and one senior student or an alumnus/alumna serving as a mentor who is committed to learning the Bible and how to live according to its principles.

Participants referred to various reasons for why growth groups have been most formative for their spiritual life, including learning biblical values with their practical applications, having friends to share their spiritual journey, and having a mentor who is also a model in their journey. RT says that from the growth group he "absorbed" a lot of values that shaped him. It was in the growth group that he learned how to study the Bible by "understanding its content, meditating on it, and learning how to apply it." The growth group helped him learn to "incorporate" biblical principles into his "conscience," so that they influenced his daily life decisions. In this way, growth groups enabled these participants to make decisions in their student life, and later on in their career and family life, based on the biblical principles.

The limited number of members in each growth group (usually between three to five persons) enabled group members to share their life journeys. Hence, "sharing struggles" among members, which can be done even when there is no formal group meeting, became one added value of the growth group (HB). For some of them the depth-of-life sharing caused the friendships in their growth groups to continue as a supporting network for many years afterward. GT recalls:

> Our friendship, our intimate relationship with growth group friends, is one of the things that sustains us, so that if possible, we never want it to end . . . We still can be friends. Because wherever we are . . . living in different cities, having different struggles, . . . the fact that we were in the same growth group binds us. Even after many years of not meeting each other, we could quickly reconnect when we meet again.

Growth groups, which are quite common in campus ministries in Indonesia, also set the environment in which mentoring relationships occurred. Rather than a single mentoring relationship, growth groups facilitate several mentoring relationships to occur between the growth group leader and its members. At the same time, a small group leader can also become an inspiring role model for its members (SE; PK; CT).

Looking at these three functions of small groups, in facilitating indepth learning, life sharing, and mentoring relationships at the same time, it is not surprising that many participants point to small groups as one of the most important experiences in the formative phase of their spiritual journey in college years.

Growth group/small group after college years

The importance of growth groups/small groups after college years is mentioned by one third of the participants (e.g. RT; LT; GT; SE; PT). RI put a special emphasis on the essential role of the small group for vocational stewardship and contrasting it with large group meetings. She comments about large group meetings in graduate fellowship: "That is like a sweetener. I mean, it makes community more beautiful. The small community becomes more beautiful to be experienced, to be walked. Since [in that way] we know that we are not a [small] group of weird people . . . That's all, just sweetener!" (RI)

RI reflects that although she did not use the small group as a place to pour out all details of her work problems, the fact that the other group members shared the same values was significantly helpful. "We had the same values and we strengthened each other, meaning that those values are worthy to fight for in any situation!" However, she also pointed out that not every small group will automatically be helpful. It "depends on our small group friends. If our small group friends are not as committed to retaining those values, the group becomes just a refreshment, just to talk with friends from our peer group. But if they are people who strive to maintain [biblical] values, we know that those values are important to fight for."

Various types of growth group/small group after college years

For some participants, the small group is more like a mentoring group led by a more senior graduate (e.g. LT; RB). In this type of group, the role of the mentor as an inspiring model and place to consult is more emphasized. For other participants, the small group is more a mutually edifying group without a mentor (e.g. RT; RI; WI). Besides the difference based on the presence of a mentor, small groups after college years also differentiated based on whether the members have similar or diverse professional backgrounds. Among participants, RI prefers a small group with people from a similar professional background due to the similarity of language and depth of communication. Others, however, experienced strong mutual support and encouragement within a group with members from various professional backgrounds other than theirs (e.g. RT; WI, RB).

The role of growth group/small group in vocational stewardship journey

In what ways is a small group important for vocational stewardship journey? There are several answers to this question which were described by the participants, including as a place to support their spiritual growth, to learn biblical values for their vocational journey, and for mutual support.

Small groups after college years could become a support for spiritual growth. For SE, the small group helped him to keep growing in faith after his college years. "I have small group friends, my [previous] small group leader. We keep in contact and keep guard of each other. For me that is what keeps me growing. Growing in my understanding of faith and growing in my learning spirit." RB has a small group leader who was a very inspiring model of a Christian worker and reflects that small group meetings became a constant source of encouragement in his vocational journey. "Often, I was apathetic. But whenever I came home from a small group meeting, I felt energized." He was often encouraged not to give up easily in facing tough challenges in his workplace.

Small groups after college years can also become a place to learn the biblical values of work from close interaction with a group leader who has experienced it longer, as well as with other group members. For example, LT says, "Through our conversation in small group, I learned that we should not divide between secular and sacred." Through learning how her small group leader worked to fully integrate his faith into his work life, she was helped to develop a holistic perspective on her own life. "Gradually my concepts changed, especially after I joined an alumni small group."

Small groups after college years can also become a place for mutual support to pray for and encourage each other (SE; PT; GT; RT; RI). RT and RI particularly stressed that small groups are the source of mutual encouragement to be faithful in their mission. "I do not share everything with them . . . But at least, we have the same values and we strengthen each other in the sense that we remind each other that the values are worthy to fight for in whatever situation!" (RI).

Some participants emphasized the crucial role of small groups in their transitional years during the first few years after college (RT; LT; GT). Based on his own experience, RT stressed that the importance of the small group started during college and continued through graduation and up to five to ten years afterwards. "I was thankful that I had a strong small group. I was thankful that I was in the same small group [with some people I appreciate]. My first five years in Jakarta I met them. And they are serious people, living deliberately. We walked whatever we talked." The group became a valuable place for mutual encouragement of their own vocational journey. GT also underlined the importance of small groups for alumni, especially in their life transition into their work life and married life:

> Alumni small groups are very urgent. Church small groups are already very helpful. However, being in the same small group with alumni who have more or less the same struggles, within the same age frame of 25–40, is very urgent. There are so many life dynamics, ups and downs, decision making, life choices, and difficulties within that age frame. If we don't have friends with whom we could pray together, it would be so hard.

Similar to earlier testimonies of the lasting relationship of the small group formed in college years, lasting relationships among the members of a small group after college years also happened. "In situations where we are facing difficulties, we need a place where we can share our struggles. I am thankful that even though my small group is not meeting anymore, we are still in touch with each other, still very close. We still maintain the relationship" (RT). The deep relationships developed in small groups can remain as a long-lasting support network in the vocational stewardship journey, beyond the limitations of the physical group meetings.

Local Church

In contrast to the significant emphasis on the importance of the faith community by the participants in this study, a relatively very weak influence of local churches was indicated in their formative years in college. Even worse, most participants declined to comment when they were asked whether their local churches had supported them sufficiently in their journey to fulfill God's calling in their work lives.

Local church in pre-college years

There were a few participants that referred to the significance of their local churches in laying the foundation for their spirituality in their late pre-college years (IT; WI; TO). The influences vary, including the basics of Christian faith and values, studying the Bible, and ministry skills. IT, for example, owed her faith and biblical values to her church pastors. "They were the ones who planted values . . . They planted faith. I think they were the ones who taught me . . . High school through college years, they were the ones who planted. I think their role [in this] was very significant."

WI also benefited from her youth counselors within the church that she joined in her high school years. The multicultural situation in that church prepared her for deep involvement with similar multicultural situations in her vocation. She also appreciates the depth of Bible learning that her counselors inspired in her teenage years. "We had the William Barclay [New Testament commentaries] series. So, our Bible Study was very inductive. When people says about O-I-A [i.e., steps in Inductive Bible Study: observation, interpretation, application] we learned that in our high school years."

Local church in college years

There were also a few participants who referred to the importance of their local churches in preparing them for their vocational stewardship journey in the college years (IT; TO; DC). IT felt that she was equipped through her role as a Sunday school teacher in her church throughout her college years. TO recalled that during his high school and college years, it was his pastor who became his mentor and model for him in, preparing him with pastoral skills for his future pastoral role as a teacher for high school students. For example, through joining the pastor in regular church visitations to its members, he learned that "receiving attention is a need." From his pastor he learned how to respond to different situations encountered during the visitations.

DC is quite an exception among the participants. Although DC was familiar with different campus ministries, during his college years he benefitted more from the biblical teaching he received from church for his spiritual foundation and also for his vocational journey. He recalled that "it was through expository preaching. At the time it was on the book of Romans . . . It was so eye opening. Eventually I learned basic doctrines from [this pastor's] series of doctrinal teaching . . . I became more aware that to work is not just about getting money, but there is calling." He adds, "I changed a lot. My concept of time, calling, cultural mandate. I received a lot from reformed theology."

Local church after college years

As mentioned earlier, most participants declined when they were asked whether their local churches had supported them sufficiently in their journey to fulfill God's calling in their work lives. Most of them kindly and generously said that they come to church to give, to contribute, to serve, not to take (e.g. PT; YI; TB; RI; MM). Some of them, like YI and PT, have even actively served as church elders for many years. When asked about his church's support for his vocational journey, YI says firmly, "No. We are the one to give. The way I see it, the effect on me is not significant. To me, our role as alumni in the church is more meaningful. Perhaps my friends . . . will answer differently if you ask. But to me, we give to the church, [not the other way around]." PT also indicated a similar experience with his church: "On lesser frequency, our church friends also sometimes visit each other. On these occasions they pray for us, for our work. This kind of support from church friends is not very significant. What I have in mind, in my concept, is that when we go to church or to a fellowship, we come to give, not to get." Similarly, RI, while firmly declining her church's involvement in her vocational journey, also politely qualifies that this might not be the case in other churches:

> Oh, no, not the church. The church is not a place where I am equipped, but a place where I contribute. Not the church, definitely. I mean, maybe it's only my church, not all churches. I know some churches have strong teachings, and therefore equipping the congregation. However, unfortunately, the church where I am a member is not a church like that.

A few others give kind excuses or explain practical reasons for why their church does not support their vocational stewardship journey. MI, whose work in politics is impacting churches nationwide, simply says that he is too introverted to explain his work to his home church. CP feels the disconnection is from herself since she does not actively participate in her home church beyond coming to Sunday Service. When asked whether her home church has been a supporting community in her vocational journey, WI says that she has minimal connection with her home church since she travels often in her work as a trainer:

> I dare not say that the church does not support, because I got away from the church. Got away not because of I was hurt, but for practical reasons. I am seldom here on Sundays. I rarely stay in one city. I have no choice. It's practical. When I'm out of town, like in Bali last week, in Ternate the week before that, what am I to do? It is not possible for me to stay in a family all the time. To me, church is family. But do they have no role? I think persons in the church still have their role [to support].

Other than the fact that local churches simply have not given sufficient attention to support their members in their work lives, TS, who has actively served in his home church for more than thirty years, indicated that talking about work in connection with faith is simply uncommon. "I am lonely. People my age do not understand what I am talking about . . . With people my age, we will not talk about Christianity like this, even though we are Christians. We would talk business!" The good news is that, even though he could not find a supporting network among other Christian professionals or businesspeople in his home church, he still can find a connection to talk about faith and work issues with some young clergy in his church.

Among the participants in this study, there was only a very rare exception mentioning a positive contribution of their local church to their vocational stewardship. TG is an example for this exception. He felt encouraged by the sermons he heard during the Sunday services. He also learned from some good programs organized in his church, such as a series of small-group discussion on the "Purpose Driven Life" book, and brought some of the ideas to be applied in his workplace. He says,

> Often, I take notes of sermons that I listen to. So, I always write it down, thankful for God's grace. I think this strengthened me. I hang on to it. There is a forty days of purpose program at church and I think it's very good. In the forty days of purpose

we get a lot of things. To the point that I'm organizing [similar] event at my workplace.

Active Service in Faith Community

Although most participants in this study said that they did not receive sufficient support from their local churches for their vocational journey, one third of the participants highly regarded their active service in local church and parachurch ministries as significantly empowering them in their vocational stewardship journey. They were able to do it mostly through learning from similar commitment to take ministry responsibilities while they were involved in campus ministries or local churches.

Active service in faith community during college years

Active involvement through ministry responsibilities was a formative experience for participants, particularly in shaping skills and character necessary for their vocational stewardship journey (e.g. PK; TB; SE; LT). Participants' experiences include their responsibilities in planning, organizing, and leading various faith community events and other businesses. For SE, for example, his organizational experiences and leadership training that he received in his campus ministry were particularly useful in the early stages of his career. "My organizational experience in campus ministry was such a stepping stone for me because it helped me develop my abilities beyond the technical and basic knowledge that I had." For LT, her involvement in various committees during her college years was a wonderful preparation for her present role as a professor in guiding her students through their organizational activities. Various types of ministry responsibilities in their college years helped the participants gain "soft skills" for their work life.

In the church context, TO learned from his involvement on his church team in caring for the poor and the sick. IT enjoyed her role as a Sunday school teacher which was healthy for her own spiritual life. Referring to the weekly preparation before the teaching ministry on Sundays she siad, "Before I feed the children, I was fed first."

The participants' commitment to take on active service responsibilities was beneficial for them in many ways. It was beneficial not only for their own spiritual growth during their college years, but also for the development of skills, values, character, and disciplines they would need when they entered the work life.

Active service in faith community after college years

As mentioned earlier, even though most participants said that they did not receive sufficient support from their home church for their vocational journey, one third of the participants highly regarded their active service in local churches and parachurch ministries as positively influential to their journey of vocational stewardship. Several explanations which come from their reflections are related with the message that they preach or teach, their identity and their alertness. For example, PK said that a preaching or teaching ministry related with work and vocation issues benefitted himself to learn even deeper:

> When I have to talk about calling, life purpose, work, I have to do a preparation. In those preparation times I usually find [something]. You know, when I have to talk, I am forced to think about it. In this way new ideas and new commitments appear more often. That's why I love to speak in workplace fellowships or graduate fellowships. I love to talk about any themes concerning alumni, even though I do not know from which book or from which source I will get the material, I know I will get it. That really, really shaped me!

Some other participants referred to a broader principle that in preaching or teaching ministries they are the ones who are "refreshed" or "fed" at the first place (RB; DC; RI; IT). "When we become a speaker, once we open the Bible we are the first to be reproved. Sometimes we are refreshed first before we even speak" (RB).

For FG, a politician, serving at student conferences and other events at faith communities became a constant reminder of his identity and mission. "The reason I like to come to such places is because it reminds me of how I used to be. It refreshes me. I know I'm not an angel. When I'm starting to stray off the road, by coming to such places, seeing the atmosphere, I recommitted myself once again." Similarly, for RB, serving in his church keeps him spiritually awake and keeps his own "fire" burning. DC consistently led a small group for young doctors and did a few other teaching and preaching ministries in the midst of his heavy workload as an internist. He reflected that all those ministry responsibilities have positively motivated him "to become an example. I have to live more carefully. [I believe] ministry is also a means of God's grace to help us grow."

Perhaps RT's reflection sums up well the positive influences of active service in faith communities to the vocational stewardship journey:

> Not because I am served, but because I'm involved, doing something. Whether it's being in a committee, creating a concept, we are forced to think. As we are thinking, our spiritual muscles are being strengthened. We are kept alert. Keep thinking, keep praying, guarding the sanctity of life so that we are used by God. I am happy to be involved in Perkantas and my church. I could start from small things, evangelism, counseling, teaching Sunday school. I was a Sunday school teacher for twenty years. Those involvements helped me privately to stay alert, vigilant, and battle-ready. And in my experience, after evaluating it, it helped me!

Non-Faith Community

Other than family and various kinds of faith communities, workplace and professional communities outside faith communities are also mentioned as positive contributions to the preparation and actual vocational stewardship journey. Most participants worked in a religiously diverse workplace, often within a context where Christians are minorities. Thus, for most of them, engaging with non-Christians in their work life is out of question. As presented earlier, a few participants referred to non-Christians as their supporting friends, and even models and mentors in their vocational journey (WI; TG; RI). Besides individual roles, non-faith based communities can also become empowering communities for the vocational stewardship journey, through shared values, skills storage, or shared concern and support for the common good (e.g. RB; SE; CP; CT; LT).

For example, for RB, the company where he previously worked inspired him with their stated values that to a certain extent shaped the work life in that company. He adopted those values into the company that he established with some of his non-Christian colleagues in the previous company.

"Professionalism, honesty, hard work, respect, and self-development. We encouraged these values to [our employees]." For SE, besides his leadership in the Christian workplace fellowship, he also perceived the importance of developing relationships and cooperation with non-Christian colleagues who have similar concerns at the workplace as part of empowering communities for his vocational stewardship journey.

Professional societies, such as journalist societies or scientific communities, are also considered to be important for professional development and a community to contribute. For CP, a journalist association helped her to catch up with journalism skills and maintain connection with other journalists. For CT, other than the significant role of faith communities, as a researcher and educator, a non-faith community such as the scientific community is part of empowering communities for his vocational stewardship journey:

> I also have scientific community. Not just faith community . . . I am also an executive member of Masyarakat Iktiologi Indonesia [=Indonesian Ichthyology Community]. In this scientific community we have our own journal. Our journal is already accredited by Dikti [=Indonesian higher education authorities]. One of the best in Indonesia. So, our scientific understanding is increasing through this community. In this way I'm [professionally] not off track, but more focused on this scientific community and contribute there.

However, as underlined in LT's assertion, in their role as part of empowering communities for vocational stewardship journey, there are also limitations of communities outside the biblical-based community:

> Community could be our office community [in a non-Christian environment]. I used to be very close to my boss. We often hang out, share each other's problems. But to me there's a limitation. He has his own values. In terms of general values like you should not deceive people, we have to be honest, etc., he has it. But I think we as Christians have more than that. Not just those norms.

The fourth category of the findings presented was about various empowering communities for participants in their vocational stewardship preparation and actual journey. These empowering communities were divided into three basic types: family, faith community, and non-faith community. Faith community was the most dominant among the three types. Empowering communities, in which empowering relationships are embedded, are crucial as a mentoring and supporting community in the various phases of vocational stewardship journey.

Figure 2 provides a summary of key aspects in vocational stewardship development and resources as described by Indonesian Christian professionals in this study. The four phases could be divided into two periods: preparational (introductory and formative phases) and actual (transitional and generative phases). The process could be seen from the phases of vocational stewardship development, as compared to the psychological-physical development. Suitable resources for each phase can be identified and compared to suitable resources in other phases.

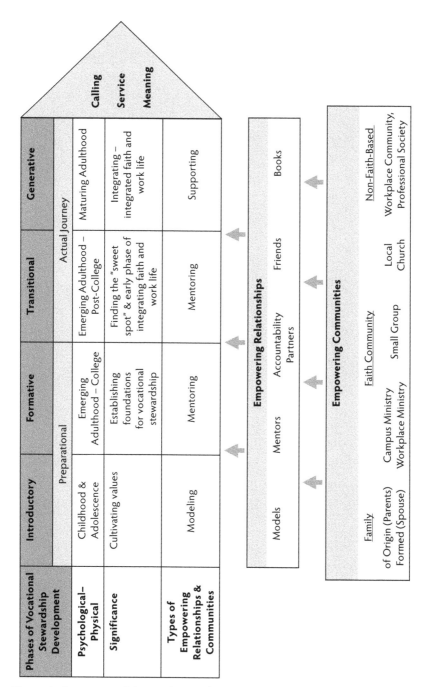

Figure 2. Summary of the Findings: The Development of Vocational Stewardship among Indonesian Christian Professionals

CHAPTER 5

Discussions and Implications

The purpose of this research was to explore the development of vocational stewardship among Indonesian Christian professionals. The research questions guided the inquiry into the description of Indonesian Christian professionals on their vocational stewardship, the significance of their college years for the development of their vocational stewardship, and the development of vocational stewardship after their college years.

This chapter consists of four parts. First, a summary of the findings presented in chapter 4. Second, a discussion on the findings in light of relevant literature. Third, implications for practice. Fourth, suggestions for further research.

Summary of the Findings

Chapter 4 presented research findings from the interviews of twenty-eight participants in this study. The findings consisted of four major categories: (1) Dimensions of Vocational Stewardships, (2) Development of Vocational Stewardship, (3) Empowering Relationships, and (4) Empowering Communities.

The first category contained participants' descriptions of their vocational stewardship journey. Vocational stewardship has multiple dimensions: first, the meaning of their work related with their perception on the connection between their work and God's work; second, their identity as a worker related with their strong sense of calling; and third, a strong orientation to serve others through their work accompanying their sense of calling.

The second category contained four phases of development in most participants' vocational stewardship journey: first, the introductory phase in pre-college years; second, the formative phase in college years; third, the transitional phase in their first few years after college; and lastly, the generative phase in the rest of their working years. This pattern of development is particularly true for participants with campus ministry background. Most participants without campus ministry background did not indicate a clear pattern of development, particularly in their college years and within a few years afterward.

The third category contained various types of empowering relationships for participants during various periods of their vocational preparation and actual journey. These empowering relationships were described more specifically by the roles of their models, mentors, accountability partners, friends, and books read in their vocational journey. These relationships are embedded in various types of communities. However, since the roles of these communities in the vocational stewardship preparation and journey are beyond merely facilitating these relationships, the empowering communities were presented separately in the fourth section.

The last category of the findings contains various types of empowering communities for a vocational stewardship journey. These empowering communities can be described as three basic types: family, faith based, and non-faith based. The faith community, which is most often referred to as an empowering community, was divided more specifically into various types: specific age/stage faith communities (youth ministry, campus ministry, and workplace ministry), growth groups/small groups, and local churches. Active service across various faith communities was also described in a separate section due to its significance.

Discussions

Called to Serve

The Centrality of Calling

Miroslaf Volf argues that the concept of vocation that Martin Luther suggested does not fit the modern work settings.[1] Volf maintains that the idea

---

1. Volf, *Work in the Spirit.*

of "station" attached to the vocational framework was suitable for the static agricultural society at the time of reformation, but not for the dynamic industrial and informational work life. Instead, Volf argues that the idea of charisma (gifts) is more suitable for the modern work setting in which people work more than one job at the same time and change jobs throughout their life time.

In line with Lee Hardy and many other scholars, and against Volf, the findings in this study suggest that the concept of vocation is still suitable and even central for participants who work as professionals in their dynamic industrial and informational work settings.[2] Most of the time, without solicitation from the researcher, participants shared their conviction of calling when asked why they chose their particular work field. This conviction is accompanied by specific accounts of how they found their calling and the affirmations they received when they were ready to give up while facing very tough challenges in their vocational journey. The findings of this study suggest that even though the participants experienced certain periods of exploration, particularly in their transitional years, many of them finally decided to stay long-term in a particular work field, or even an institution that they perceived as their calling. By contrast, the findings in the literature suggest that gift(s) are only one among several factors, including the needs of others, passion, and opportunities, by which participants find the "sweet spot" of their calling.

Why is the notion of calling important? First, beyond discourses on work, calling places our life stories in a larger story, a biblical meta-narrative in which the Creator has called human beings to participate in the fulfillment of his story. Second, in contrast to the temptation of self-authorship in the emphasis on the giftedness, calling suggests the submission of our vocational journey to the Main Author of the larger story of this world. At times, the life stories of the participants illustrated this point clearly. Often they chose certain challenging work fields not because of their heroism or altruism, but because of their submission to what they understand as God's calling. Third, calling helps us to see work from a wider perspective. As Luther suggested, calling includes all types of human relationships, whether domestic

---

2. Hardy, *Fabric*; see also Guinness, *The Call*; Schuurman, *Vocation*; Keller and Alsdorf, *Every Good Endeavor*.

or social, paid or unpaid work. The findings of this study show how some participants indicated a strong sense of calling for their roles as parents, and how they found the "sweet spot" by valuing both work life and family life. Fourth, calling also means that we are not on our own for its fulfillment. The findings of this study illustrate this point strongly. The participants told how they experienced affirmation and provision in hard times beyond their own capability to handle the situations.

In conclusion, calling is central in vocational stewardship since it put human beings, as workers, in connection with the Creator, in whose story and by whose mandate they can find the meaning and purpose of their work and their lives.

Calling and Service as Two Double Sides of a Coin

Literature suggests that closely attached to the idea of calling is service. As Luther suggests, God's vocation, manifested in various kinds of human work, is the "mask" through which God cares for us. Or in other words, "Human life is to be lived out in society in mutual service and support."[3]

In accordance with the literature, the findings of this study indicate that the strong conviction of calling in most participants is accompanied by a strong orientation of service in their work notably for society and the under-privileged. The fact that they come from various professional backgrounds – only a few of them work in "service professions" (e.g. doctor, educator) and non-profit organizations – highlights the point even more. It underlines the principle that the dividing line of vocational stewardship is not profit versus non-profit, or the sacred versus the secular institution. The dividing line is whether a worker has a restored vision of work. As Guinness aptly says, "Our gifts are ultimately God's, and we are only 'stewards' – responsible for the prudent management of property that is not our own. This is why our gifts are always 'ours for others,' whether in the community of Christ or the broader society outside, especially the neighbor in need."[4]

Service is very closely attached to vocation. Through the "creation man-date" (Gen 1:27–28) God called us to serve others and the created world as his stewards, for his glory. At the heart of fallen human nature is the reversal

---

3. Hardy, *Fabric*, 60.
4. Guinness, *The Call*, 47.

of the orientation of work toward self-serving, at the expense of others and the created world, often by trying to manipulate God for this purpose. It was Christ's redemption that enabled those who follow him to have a restored orientation of work, by which work can be placed within the larger picture of our essential task to love God and others in our whole life (Matt 22:36–40). Thus, calling, from a biblical perspective, always means calling to serve others and the rest of creation for God's glory.

Between the Instrumental and Intrinsic Meaning of Work

Literature on the theology of work often emphasizes the dualistic perspective of sacred-secular work as the center of the problem that prevents Christians from seeing the intrinsic meaning of their work (see Cosden's, *The Heavenly Good for Earthly Work*, for instance). Amy Sherman's 2011 research on a number of marketplace ministries and Christian professional societies also indicates that emphasis on the instrumental meaning of work only as a vehicle for evangelism, which is closely related to this dualistic perspective, abounds.[5] This thinking seems to have perpetuated more books and articles written to counter this narrow perspective.

The findings of this study, even though based on selected participants, suggest that a purely instrumental meaning of work coupled with a dualistic perspective of sacred-secular work is still around. A few participants seemed to still hold this perspective. However, the findings also suggest that there is another challenge to understanding the meaning of work. Among Christian professionals perhaps the biggest challenge it is not the problem of a purely instrumental or dualistic perspective. The majority of participants in this study valued both the intrinsic and instrumental meaning of their work for the ministry of the gospel. The problem seems to lie in the way they embraced both meanings in a conceptually integrated framework. Some of them seemed to have been able to embrace both the "cultural mandate" and the "gospel mandate" as a holistic mission or within an integrated framework (e.g. DC; YI; LT; RI; YM). However, some others seemed to still struggle with how to put the two meanings together. For example, in one of his statements, PT asserts that his work as a home builder/developer is meaningful in creating a new neighborhood and that his work reflects God's character

---

5. Sherman, *Kingdom Calling*.

as Creator. However, in another statement he also mentioned that at one point he struggled on the meaning of his work as a homebuilder as worldly and found an answer later on knowing that some of the shop houses he built were later used for church premises.

Although more data is still needed to confirm the comparison, those who have a conviction of calling based on a solid understanding of the intrinsic meaning of their work tend to be more eager and resilient in fulfilling the mission through their work. A deeply rooted belief of the intrinsic meaning of their work accompanied by a holistic perspective of calling also impacted their decision making, such as in facing the dual responsibilities of work and family. RI, for instance, finally decided to resign from her first job which she loved wholeheartedly after she had a baby. Although she was still struggling about whether her present job, which was less time-consuming, was the best choice, she valued both her calling in the public place through her work and her parental calling for her toddler:

> Honestly, I'm not too sure. I mean, [my present work] is only a middle ground. What can bridge my commitment to keep contributing to this country in a public place? Of course being a stay at home mom can also contribute to it, but up to this time I believe that I am called to contribute in the public space, to this country, but in which I can also maintain my family.

These are three dimensions of vocational stewardship that emerge from the findings of this study: calling, service, and meaning of work. Looking closer at the life stories of the participants, it will become more obvious that these three dimensions of vocational stewardship involves the whole personhood: up, in, and out;[6] knowledge, value system, and behavior[7]; or heart, mind, body, social relations, and soul.[8] This suggests that only a spiritual formation that transforms the whole personhood will enable a person to fulfill his or her vocational stewardship. Perhaps Amy Sherman's description on the *tsadiqqim* would be most helpful for this purpose.

---

6. Sherman.
7. Dettoni, "Psychology of Adulthood."
8. Willard, "Spiritual Formation."

Attending Vocational Stewardship Development in Each Phase

The Crucial Formative Phase

Parks' seminal work, *Big Questions Worthy Dreams,* and also Garber's empirical research on the impact of college life,[9] among other writings, suggest emerging adulthood as a crucial period in the process of human meaning-making, which has enormous implications for the rest of adulthood years. The findings of this study, looking at emerging adulthood as one of the periods in the development of vocational stewardship in Christian professionals, affirm this claim. On the other hand, literature also helps to explain the findings.

The research findings suggest that the formative phase in the college years is crucial for the development of vocational stewardship of Christian professionals. If well taken care of, the formative phase set the foundation and basic framework needed for a thriving/generative vocational stewardship. The findings suggest that earlier age serve more as an introductory for this formative phase, in which basic values are being cultivated, mostly through the role of parents and significant others in the family. Only a few outliers experienced a seemingly early formative period in their high school years. On the other hand, although a follow-up in the transitional phase in post-college years also need to be well-taken care of, the degree of its importance is not as high as in the formative phase. This transitional phase could also be seen as an extension of this formative phase in an almost totally new context, of work and marriage life. Afterward, there seems to be no single pattern of essential development that these Christian professionals experienced except continuing to strive to integrate their faith into their work.

The findings also suggest that those who did not experience a well taken care of formative phase tended to experience a highly unpatterned vocational stewardship development. In some cases they experienced a prolonged struggle even to make meaning of their work life, or to find an indepth connection between their Christian faith and their work life. Thus, the research findings affirm that the formative phase in college, followed by a transition

---

9. Garber, *Fabric of Faithfulness.*

phase in the first few years of post-college, are crucial for a fruitful development of vocational stewardship among Christian professionals.

If Parks is correct in her claim of "the birth of critical awareness" in emerging adulthood, [10] there are important consequences emerging for our understanding of emerging adulthood as a crucial period for the development of vocational stewardship. With the birth of critical awareness in their thought structure, emerging adults now have a potentially growing capacity to critically question beliefs, values, and practices of their own, their faith community and their world. At this highly vulnerable period, they search for the meaning (big questions) and purpose of life (worthy dreams). But at the same time, they also encounter competing unworthy dreams of merely self-seeking or distorted life goals. It is precisely at this phase of life that emerging adults need to be confronted with the most challenging but most worthy task in human life, that is, to participate in the great cause of the Creator by bringing the foretaste of his shalom into this world through their work and their whole life. Garber's research on university graduates seems to resonate with Park's claim and the findings of this research. In his study, a robust biblical worldview starting to develop in his subjects during their college years found to be crucially impacting the way they navigated the rest of their lives.[11]

As many empirical researchers suggest, the potential to think critically, however, does not automatically happen. It needs to be nurtured. Stephen Brookfield, a seminal thinker in critical thinking, observes that to be able to think critically about something one needs to have sufficient information and understanding about it in the first place. He suggests that for people to be able to develop their critical thinking on certain subjects, they need to master the "grammar of the subject."[12] The grammar itself contains two basic elements. First, the content grammar is the basic building block of knowledge in the respective subject. Second, the epistemological grammar is the procedure that verifies whether certain knowledge is legitimate. For emerging adults to be able to develop their critical thoughts toward issues related with their vocational stewardship, they need to learn some basic

---

10. Parks, *Big Questions*, 8

11. Garber, *Fabric of Faithfulness*.

12. Brookfield, *Teaching for Critical Thinkers*, 78.

grammar of vocational stewardship. For example, learning the theology of work will help them to think critically about the meaning and purpose of their work from the biblical perspective. Learning about holistic mission and public theology will help them to think critically about how Christians should interact with the surrounding culture and in what ways they can bring a foretaste of God's kingdom through their work. Thus, teaching the grammar of the subject in the formative phase should be one of the focuses of attention for Christian educators.

Two further thoughts should also be added here. First, literature, notably the "up, in, and out" in Sherman's outline of the biblical "*tsadiqqim,*" suggest that vocational stewardship involves more than cognitive dimension.[13] Likewise, literature on spiritual formation and developmental theories suggests that, important as it is, a person's mind or cognitive development is just one aspect of the whole personhood. The research findings reflected this well-known wisdom, both through the multiple dimensions of vocational stewardship they described and through the various aspects they referred to as foundational for their vocational stewardship journey (conversion, biblical framework, values and character, spiritual disciplines, Bible study skills, soft skills, and work field exploration). It is noteworthy that when they have settled the question of meaning and purpose of their work life, mostly in their formative and transition phases, their struggle in the rest of their vocational stewardship journey is more filled with the themes of wisdom, compassion, courage, endurance, and discipline in navigating through complex situations in the workplace and society. Therefore, the best way to prepare Christian professionals for a generative vocational stewardship journey is through a spiritual formation that forms the whole of their personhood with a solid and thorough foundation in their formative years.

Second, as literature suggests, including Parks, Setran and Kiesling, and Garber, it is important to have the presence of more mature persons who take up the role of mentor-model to help emerging adults navigate through unknown new horizons.[14] Beyond the presence of a mentor-model, the findings suggest the importance of the presence of a network of empowering

---

13. Sherman, *Kingdom Calling.*
14. Parks, *Big Questions*; Setran and Kiesling, *Spiritual Formation*; Garber, *Fabric of Faithfulness.*

relationships that includes but is not limited to the role of mentor-model. In agreement with Parks' suggestion of the importance of a mentoring community in emerging adulthood, the research findings also suggest that more than the network of empowering relationships is needed. Looking at the multidimensional tasks in the formative phase that has been discussed earlier, it is not a surprise that the empowering community with all the dynamics within it is needed for a holistic spiritual transformation to prepare for the vocational stewardship journey. We will discuss further the themes of empowering relationships and empowering community in the following sections.

Exploration in the Transitional Phase

Literature on emerging adulthood tends to treat this period as a life-span without significant division within it. The findings in this study suggest that to be able to understand better and hence to help emerging adults better, a clearer boundary between college life and post-college life should be considered. At least for the social context in Indonesia, college life is quite different from work life, even in their first few years of work. Geographically, most of them experience changes, since many of them work in a different city than where they studied, and therefore they need to adjust into new community contexts. Socially, they encounter a totally different set of expectations and responsibilities, compared to when they were students. In accordance with these major changes the research findings suggest that this is a period marked by intense adjustments into the new context of work life, often followed by married life. All of these significantly different situations demand special attention for a new college graduate.

Therefore, it is not surprising that the research findings suggest another phase after the formative phase in college years as important for the development of vocational stewardship within these Christian professionals. This transitional phase is marked by the two main activities of finding the sweet spot of calling and an early phase of integrating their faith into their work life. Both could not be done earlier in their college years. Although early processes of exploration should have been started in their college years, the findings suggest that they still explore choices by hands-on experience up to five to ten years of working. Some of them claim that the previous work experiences in other fields or work settings served as a preparation for their long-term work in the field they claim as their calling.

Therefore, the findings of this study suggest that to be able to understand and help emerging adults in their development of vocational stewardship, Christian educators should also give special attention to more specific needs of emerging adults in their transitional phase during the first few years post-college. In a way, this transitional phase could also be seen as an extended formative phase, but in a completely different context from the college life. Two participants in this study who did not have sufficient formative experiences in their college years benefited from formative experiences, empowering relationships, and empowering communities in their first few years after they graduated (IT, WI). The result was significantly positive for their vocational stewardship journey. On the other hand, as one participant stressed, he observed that without sufficient attachment to empowering relationships and empowering communities in this transitional phase, many of his friends drifted away in their vocational journey (SE).

Shift in the Generative Phase

The research findings suggest that several types of change occurred as a person moved from the transitional phase to the generative phase. First, the shift from the early phase of integrating faith and work, marked by the question of whether their faith is workable in the newly entered work life and in what ways, to the later phase of intentionally integrating faith and work, marked by questioning whether they could fully integrate their beliefs and values into increasingly complex responsibilities and the wider impact of their work within the world of diverse and competing values. Within the generative phase itself there seems to be another move in the later years to a seemingly more settled position, at least in concept and conviction of integrating their faith and their work. Second, is the shift from striving to find the sweet spot of their calling to the striving to stay faithful and to be fruitful in their calling. Third, is the shift of empowering relationships from dependent support to mutual support. While it is hard to define when a person moves from the transitional phase to the generative phase, mostly due to variability in personality and context for each person, the difference between the two phases could be affirmed from a developmental perspective such as in the third shift, in the type of empowering relationships at work.

Parks identifies the shift of the form of relationship from fragile inner-dependence in emerging adulthood to confident inner-dependence in tested adulthood.[15] She suggests that if the fragile inner-dependence in emerging adulthood is met with encouragement and confirmation, over time this form of dependence will shift to a confident inner-dependence. "The more tested adult has a deepened capacity to compose his or her sense of value and promise and has become strong enough to let the mentor be otherwise – even to have feet of clay."[16] However, they still need others, but in a different way, "as the emerging adult becomes more fully adult, mentors can become peers in significant ways."[17]

Very interestingly, the findings of this study coincide well with Parks' description of the shift from what she called fragile inner-dependence in emerging adulthood to the confident inner-dependence in tested adulthood. The research findings suggest that after the transition phase is over, the long period of the generative phase is marked by a significant change in the type of relationship with the significant others. Previous mentors gradually become accountability partners. Mutual support from a spouse also increasingly becomes more important and replaces the need of a mentor. Even further, the awareness and intention to take the role of a mentor and model in the lives of others is also increasing. This suggests a drastically different approach is needed in helping Christian professionals to thrive in this phase. Forms of mutually supporting relationships, instead of mentoring relationships, need to be developed. Perhaps what should be promoted is a different set of community dynamics, through which they can take more active and generative roles.

Christian professionals in the generative phase keep needing others for mutual support. From the perspective of learning, they also need to learn to deal with new and increasing challenges in their vocational stewardship journey. However, the shift from dependent relationships to mutual types of relationships suggests a different approach of learning and support suitable for them. Here Knowles' andragogy principles should be taken more into account. Perhaps, of the six principles that he promoted, three of them

---

15. Parks, *Big Questions*.
16. Parks.
17. Parks, 109.

would be most helpful for this purpose. Adult learners (1) bring a growing reservoir of experience as a source of learning; (2) learn to cope with real-life situations, especially in changing developmental stages; and (3) are problem-oriented, instead of subject-oriented in their learning.[18]

Knowles is correct in saying that adults bring to the learning table their rich life experience. Most likely, those experiences have contributed to their beliefs and values. However, as John Dewey asserts, bare experience is not adequate for effective learning. Even though "all genuine education comes about through experience," some experiences are "miss-educative," producing biases that hinder further growth.[19] It is true that even "effective learning does not follow from a positive experience but from effective reflection."[20] Likewise, in learning for further development of vocational stewardship, past experiences need to be critically examined from a biblical perspective. Thus, for fruitful learning in the generative phase, critical reflection skills and habits are required. This suggests that critical reflection skills should be taught as part of the "grammar" of vocational stewardship and the habits should be cultivated early in the formative phase. By the time Christian professionals rely on their confident inner-dependence, the critical reflection skills and habits would be even more important to their learning.

Knowles is also correct in saying that for adult learners their immediate concerns and problems often become the focus of their learning. However, as bare experience could be without critical reflection, mere concern or problem-oriented learning might not be fruitful. Along with increasing vocational power (expertise, position, influence, etc.,)[21] as Christian professionals navigate through the generative phase, with increasing challenges and complexities of the problems in bringing the foretaste of God's kingdom, to pick up a few examples, it took more than bare experience and concern to understand the problems of commonly practiced corruption and legalized migrant workers. It required a critical lens to understand the roots of the problem, so that creative and strategic solutions for the problem can be promoted (RT; TB). Effective learning in the generative phase requires

---

18. Knowles, Holton, and Swanson, *Adult Learner*.
19. Dewey, *Experience and Education*, 13.
20. Merriam, Caffarella and Baumgartner, *Learning in Adulthood*, 145.
21. Sherman, *Kingdom Calling*, 121

critical reflections that examine beliefs, values, and assumptions that affect the way we make sense of our experiences. This is what Mezirow specified as "premise reflection," which he differentiates from "content reflection" (thinking about the actual experience itself) and "process reflection" (thinking about problem-solving strategies).[22]

Furthermore, for the purpose of faith and work integration, besides critical reflection skills, sufficient familiarity with biblical and theological knowledge is also required. Although learning the Bible is a lifelong process, for a fruitful critical reflection, sufficient grounding in basic biblical knowledge should have been acquired as part of the "grammar" of vocational stewardship in the formative phase.

For the purpose of learning that effectively includes critical reflection of experience/concern/problem, indepth interaction with the biblical values, and also using dialogical approaches in a small group setting, perhaps Groome's shared praxis approach, with dialogue and critical reflection of experiences centered in the faith tradition, can be considered as a potentially fruitful model for learning in the generative phase.[23]

A Network of Empowering Relationships

A Closer Look to Mentor

Literature suggests the important role of a mentor for spiritual formation in emerging adulthood.[24] Likewise, Garber's research on the development of vocational stewardship in college years refers to the importance of the presence of the mentor who at the same time becomes a model who embodies the values being taught.[25]

The research findings affirm the important role of both model and mentor in the formative and transitional phases of vocational stewardship development. Two thirds of the participants in this study referred to the importance of the role model for their vocational stewardship journey. Likewise, two

---

22. Mezirow, *Learning as Transformation*; see also Merriam, Caffarella and Baumgartner, *Learning in Adulthood*, 145.

23. Groome, *Sharing Faith*.

24. E.g., Parks, *Big Questions*; Dunn and Sundene, *Shaping the Journey*; and Setran and Kiesling, *Spiritual Formation*.

25. Garber, *Fabric of Faithfulness*.

thirds of the participants also referred to the important role of mentor. The presence of more mature people as mentors who at the same time can also become a model of vocational stewardship is considered to be crucial in helping participants to have their spiritual foundations built and to navigate through uncharted territories in the first years of their work life and married life.

Setran and Kiesling suggest that the role of mentor for emerging adults is "to envision and model adult belief and responsibility . . . bringing them to a sense of continual and humble reliance on the work of God in and around them" through fostering attentiveness to God's work in the past, present, and future.[26] Parks suggests that the key roles of a mentor are "recognition, support, challenge, and inspiration—in ways that are accountable to the life of the emerging adult."[27]

The research findings suggest that to better understand the role of mentor in vocational stewardship development, the role of mentor in the formative phase (in college life) should be differentiated from the role of mentor in the later phases (in work life). In the formative phase the role of mentor mostly is helping them to develop the foundation of their spirituality, helping them understand their calling, and becoming a role model for them. Most mentors these participants referred to in their college years were their growth group leaders, including more senior students, a few graduates, and campus ministry workers.

In the post-college years, the role of a mentor was most significant in the transitional phase. Mentor roles included inspiration (through their insights and model), encouragement (in facing hard times in walking through their calling), feedback or "mirror" (especially important in navigating through grey areas, such as in political field), affirmation (from experienced and mature thoughts to the fragile young minds), and support (through their prayer, advice, etc.). Most mentors in post-college years were more senior Christian professionals and also a few full-time ministers.

By comparing and contrasting the findings with the two descriptions of the roles of mentor, several overlaps can be identified including

---

26. Setran and Kiesling, *Spiritual Formation*, 238.
27. Parks, *Big Questions*, 167.

inspiration-modeling, support-encouragement, and recognition-affirma-tion.[28] Perhaps an important element of the findings missing from the two descriptions is feedback or "mirror." This element appears in other adult learning literature as an essential element in fostering critical reflection.[29]

Appreciating Model

Besides the role of mentor, the research findings also expand our horizon to give sufficient attention to the importance of a model in vocational steward-ship development. This study reveals a variety of roles attached to a model, apart from what a mentor can do, and also the existence of a model as a separate entity from mentor.

A living model is considered to be significant in helping participants to learn from rich, three-dimensional embodied values beyond two-dimen-sional words in textbooks or abstract concepts. Models inspire participants in this study with their dedicated spirit, commitment in the midst of tough challenges, passion for social justice, and various kinds of living examples of vocational stewardship. In certain cases, this encounter is not just inspir-ing; it is even transforming. In MI's case, he initially did not even think of returning to Indonesia after having a college education abroad. His decision to devote his life for his country was triggered by his encounter with some Indonesian professors who did their graduate studies in the same university as his and were wholeheartedly willing to return to Indonesia to serve their home country.

Models that participants in this study referred to are not limited to their mentors. They include historical figures, significant others in their upbringing, and people they encountered in their faith community, some-times outside the faith community, who embodied vocational stewardship values. They do not necessarily have similar professional background with the participants.

A Wider Network of Relationships Needed

The fact that models are important and that they are not necessarily mentors suggests the importance of a wider network of empowering relationships

---

28. Setran and Kiesling, *Spiritual Formation*; Parks, *Big Questions*.

29. Brookfield, *Developing Critical Thinkers*.

instead of a single mentoring relationship as necessary for a richer vocational stewardship development. The research findings also suggest the important role of accountability partners. In college years and a few years post-college this often takes place within a small group context. In later years many participants refer to the role of their spouse, a few refer to their previous mentor and others, as their accountability or dialogue partner. Some of them also refer to the contribution of their friends and books in their vocational stewardship journey.

When all these are taken into account, our horizon is widened. The research findings suggest that for a fruitful development of vocational stewardship a network of empowering relationships is needed. This means that it takes a community, instead of a single person, to do it (in accordance with Garber's research). This community consists of more mature people who embody the values (as models) and who care for the younger generation (mentors), fellow travelers who have similar commitment (accountability partners and friends), and more loosely attached inspirers (book authors) who walk with the same hope and values. At times there are also non-Christians who share some thoughts and influences that overlap with the biblical values that would contribute in this journey.

Indeed, literature suggests that relationship is an important element in the process of "human becoming."[30] Literature also suggests that relationship, as one among other components of community dynamic, is one among other elements of the matrix of transformation in spiritual formation.[31] For a more complete picture, we need to move one step further to explore the role of community in the vocational stewardship journey.

A Network of Empowering Community

Transformation in the Formative Phase
Literature suggests the importance of community in spiritual formation. Notably Parks' idea of a mentoring community, Setran and Kiesling's highlights of Baucum's usage of the encapsulation theory, and Rambo's matrix of transformation will be brought to frame and enrich the discussion on

---

30. Parks, *Big Questions.*
31. Rambo, *Understanding Religious Conversion.*

the research findings.[32] Their frameworks are particularly helpful as multiple lenses through which to better understand the need of empowering community in the formative and transitional phases in emerging adulthood. However, they will also be useful, with certain modifications, for further understanding of the need for an empowering community in the generative phase.

The research findings suggest that the faith community is most significantly helpful for participants' vocational stewardship preparation in college years and the actual journey in their work life. Three quarters of the participants were involved in campus ministry in their college years. For most of them their campus fellowship group became the main empowering community in their formative phase. For more than half of the participants, workplace or graduate fellowship groups also became the empowering community in their transitional phase. While active support from local churches is relatively weak, a significant number of participants referred to their ministry roles in a faith community, including local churches and parachurch organizations they joined, as significantly empowering them in their vocational journey through the generative phase. How do we explain these phenomena?

Rambo suggests four components of the matrix of transformation in spiritual formation (that he called "religious conversion"): relationships, rituals, rhetoric (including teaching, songs), and roles.[33] When the dynamic of campus ministry life is viewed with the lens of this matrix, all components seem to appear in their activities. Participants who were deeply involved in campus ministry in their college years experienced each of the four components quite intensely. They encountered models and mentors. They experienced focused learning and deep relationships in growth groups/ small groups, received biblical teaching and developed relationships through various types of large group meetings within and outside of their campus. Their values, character, and skills were also shaped and developed through ministry responsibilities and their overall community lives.

---

32. Parks, *Big Questions*; Setran and Kiesling, *Spiritual Formation*; Rambo, *Understanding Religious Conversion*.

33. Rambo, *Understanding Religious Conversion*.

From the perspective of encapsulation theory, it is also not surprising that students who were deeply involved in campus ministries also experienced intense formative years that significantly shaped their worldview and value system. Through their involvement in their campus fellowship groups they experienced physical, social, and ideological encapsulation that provided a high degree of socialization that shaped their life going forward. It is not surprising that for those who were deeply involved in their local campus fellowship group, they experienced intense formative years through their campus ministry. As one participant said, "For me, my experience in campus ministry was very influential because I went through many life-changing experiences there" (RA).

Both theories help to explain a variety of phenomena, including that (1) even though they regularly went to worship at local churches every Sunday, the most influence in their life was through their involvement in their campus fellowship community; (2) in a pioneering situation this matrix has not yet fully developed nor was the encapsulation process, therefore, a few participants who joined a campus ministry group in the pioneering stage seemed to have less significant stories to tell of their campus ministry experience; (3) a few other participants who were not involved in campus ministry but later on joined a graduate fellowship group intensely, did experience the relationships, rituals, rhetoric, and roles quite intensely in their transitional phase and seem to have experienced a late but significant formative phase in their transitional years.

Both theories also help to explain the power of community, instead of any single component in the matrix of transformation, as much more promising for a holistic spiritual formation to prepare people sufficiently for their vocational stewardship journey. Parks describes this formative community as a mentoring community. She suggests a mentoring community must have a network of belonging, big-enough questions, encounters with otherness, a key images-vision, a community of practice (hearth, table, and commons), and the development of fruitful habits of mind "that make it possible for emerging adults to hold diversity and complexity, to wrestle with moral ambiguity, and to develop deeper wells of meaning, purpose, and faith."[34]

---

34. Parks, *Big Questions*, 185.

All these suggest that the effectiveness of the formation process will depend on whether certain basic elements, as have been outlined in different ways, could be developed in the respective faith community and that a formative community is not limited to campus fellowship group setting. Each faith community, whether a local church or parachurch organization, big or small, could develop its own type of mentoring community suitable for vocational stewardship formation, according to its context.

While the need of community support is still high in the transitional phase, the nature of situations in this period is quite different from the college life. Some participants stressed time constraints that they experienced in the workplace. Some others described job changes and residential changes they experienced in this phase. In the midst of a lot of change, stress, and uncertainty, they still need a mentoring community to help them navigate through the new territories. For the need of community support in the transitional phase, the research findings suggest that many participants refer to empowering relationships developed in the form of small groups as most significant in this phase. This group is a newly formed group with new fellow graduates, with or without the presence of more senior adults who take on the role as their mentors. Perhaps in navigating through the time and geographical constraint, a small group setting is more flexible and still fulfills their needs. A faith community in the form of a workplace or graduate ministry still plays a certain role, but much less intensively compared to what they have in their college years.

As it has been discussed earlier in the "Empowering Relationships" section, the years of adulthood from the thirties onward in the generative phase is quite different from the previous two phases in emerging adulthood. The shift from the dependent type of support for a fragile inner-dependence in emerging adulthood to a mutual type of support for a confident inner-dependence in tested adulthood also bring consequences in the type of empowering community suitable in the generative phase. Most helpful to consult with among the theories discussed earlier is Rambo's matrix of transformation. Perhaps the difference is in the emphasis of which component(s) of the matrix becomes more important at this phase.

Interesting data that comes from the research findings is that even though most participants say that they did not receive intentional support (teaching, recognition, etc.) from their church for their vocational stewardship journey, at least one third of them stressed that their active service in a local church and parachurch organization was significantly empowering. They worked in a variety of roles: Sunday school teachers, small group leaders, lay preachers, and church elders. While active service in college years was perceived more as a part of their learning process, active service in post-college years was perceived more as indirectly empowering them in their vocational steward- ship journey. They explained this phenomenon in a variety of ways about their active service in a faith community, such as keeping them alert spiri- tually, refreshing their spirit, having a constant reminder of their identity and mission, and feeding themselves each time they prepared a sermon/talk (RB; DC; RI; IT; RT; FG). With their stronger impulse to give, the "role" component in the generative phase seems to play a more important part in their community engagement.

Although they did not give more specific details of their faith community as their supporting community at this phase, their active involvement in church and parachurch organizations seems to be in accordance with their impulse to develop mutual relationships and mutual learning. Perhaps their commitment to their church also indicates that the component of rituals such as Sunday worship and other church activities, serve well as a constant reminder of their identity and mission in their long-term vocational journey.

Small Group and Vocational Stewardship

Involvement in a small group has gained a wide acceptance over the past four decades as a reliable approach for spiritual formation in multiple con- texts, such as in church or parachurch settings, in both the United States and other parts of the world.[35] Various models developed in different places could be identified.[36] The significance of a small group or growth group as a form of empowering community for vocational stewardship development was referred to by a significant number of participants in this study. More than half of the participants pointed to its importance in the formative phase, and more than one third of them pointed to its importance in the transitional phase.

---

35. Donahue and Gowler, "Small Groups"; Atkinson, "Annotated Bibliography."
36. Boren and Egli, "Small Group."

The research findings affirm some benefits of a small group for vocational stewardship development. First, small group, in which membership is based on commitment (closed membership), facilitates the development of empowering relationships. Without saying that all small group leaders and members are always successful with this task, developing small groups in faith communities does facilitate the development of both mentoring relationships between the small group leaders and the members and also provides mutual support among small group members within the same group. This has proven to be very useful in the formative phase where potential mentors are usually the ones who take the initiative to form the group, and in the transitional phase, where the initiative comes from a mentor, the members, or someone in charge of developing small groups in the respective faith community.

Furthermore, the findings also suggest that these empowering relationships can continue much longer than the formal group meetings. This is very valuable in the further vocational journey during the generative phase, when they need support from people whom they know well and trust. As one participant said about his small group which shared in formal meetings many years ago in his first five years of work life, "In situations where we are facing difficulties. We need a place where we can share our struggles. I am thankful that even though my small group is not meeting anymore, we are still in touch with each other and still very close" (RT).

Second, with its dynamic dialogical setting and application-oriented approach, the small group could become very fruitful for learning. As one participant reflected, his college life growth group helped him to learn to "incorporate" biblical principles into his "conscience," through the sequential habits of understanding, meditating, and applying what he learned (RT). In this way, the growth group enabled these participants to develop the skills and habit of integrating the biblical principles into their daily life. Small groups in post-college years could also become a meaningful place to learn the biblical values of work from close interaction with a group leader and also learn from other group members. One participant said that learning how her small group leader attempted to fully integrate his faith into his work life, she was helped to develop a holistic perspective on her own life. "Gradually my concepts changed, especially after I joined an alumni small group" (LT).

As a miniature community, the dynamic within a well-run small group seems to meet most of the four components of the matrix of transformation and are effective in its encapsulation process. This may explain why a small group has been so powerful and widely used in various churches and parachurch ministries. The findings of this study affirm the importance of small groups in facilitating vocational stewardship development. A few participants in this study even emphasized the importance of the small group above other ministry approaches. As expressed by one participant, "In my opinion, growth groups hold the most importance among other activities. Larger group meetings were generally edifying, but growth group was very helpful [for me]" (HC).

However, without ignoring the fact of the power of small group, a wider look at the dynamic within a larger faith community, whether church or parachurch, suggests that a number of important elements will be missed if small groups are over emphasized. To pick up a few examples from earlier discussions, essential components will be missed from the spiritual formation process when the focus is only on small groups, such as models beyond respective small group leaders, indepth teaching beyond what the small group leader can facilitate, and various ministry roles and responsibilities in a larger community. In this case, the four components of the matrix of the transformation could be helpful for a quick cross check.

This suggests Christian educators who launch small groups, important as they are for vocational stewardship development, might benefit from seeing a larger picture of the function of a larger faith community as an empowering community for the development of vocational stewardship. Borrowing Bronfenbrenner's theoretical lens of ecology of human development, the small group method could be seen as one among other microsystems that influence spiritual formation.[37] It could even be perceived as a sub-microsystem of a local faith community (whether campus ministry, workplace ministry, or local church). Therefore, for a more robust spiritual formation for vocational stewardship development, a small group approach must be put together with other microsystems directly influencing the person's spiritual formation (the mesosystem); even further, to take into consideration indirect

---

37. Bronfenbrenner, *Ecology of Human.*

factors influencing the spiritual formation of the person (the exosystem and macrosystem). This will encourage Christian educators to have a more holistic approach in designing spiritual formation, whether for preparation or actual vocational stewardship journey of Christian professionals.

Family and Vocational Stewardship

Family could be viewed as a context for vocational stewardship. Martin Luther affirmed the biblical teaching that calling has multiple dimensions. Besides being applied to societal roles, mostly related to paid work, calling is also applied to domestic or family roles, such as a husband, wife, parents, and children. This teaching has been followed by recent authors.[38]

The research findings indicate that for female participants who were married and had children, a holistic understanding of vocation was important. At certain points in their lives they encountered difficult questions in choosing between their calling in the public sphere and their domestic calling. A holistic understanding of the multiple dimensions of vocation is helpful for the participants to negotiate between the different roles. They also found that their sweet spot could change as time goes by. For example, the demand for parental nurturing diminishes as their children pass their elementary school age so that mothers can be more flexible to refocus on their work.

On the other hand, family can also be viewed as a resource for vocational stewardship. The research findings suggest that the significant others in the family, particularly parents, have a crucial role in the introductory phase of their vocational stewardship development. It is significant that the persons that the participants referred to in the introductory phase, particularly in their own childhood, were encountered in family life. Where concrete experiences were the main venue for their learning, they learned values, such as integrity, dedication, a sense of mission, and valuing others, through what they saw, heard, and experienced in the daily family life (TS; TO; WI; LT; PT).

In the following two phases of emerging adulthood, the role of family seems to disappear. Among other possible explanations, perhaps this is also related to the sociological factor. Starting from college years, most participants live in geographically distant from where their parents live. They

---

38. E.g. Guinness, *The Call*; Placher, *Callings*; Keller and Alsdorf, *Every Good Endeavor*.

spent most of their daily life with their cohorts in the college life, with their colleagues at the workplace and perhaps also their own community outside the workplace. The role of family as resources for the vocational stewardship journey seems to reappear quite strongly in the generative phase, after they are married. About half of the participants point to the crucial role of their spouse in their vocational stewardship journey.

In one or two cases a spouse became a model or mentor. But in most cases, participants benefitted from mutual support shared with their spouse, whether as accountability partner, dialogue partner, prayer partner, or all of these kinds of supporting partnerships. In accordance with the shift from a dependent relationship in the transitional phase in emerging adulthood to a mutual relationship in the generative phase, mutual support from a spouse became one of the most important resources for the vocational stewardship journey.

These research findings on the roles of parents and spouse in the journey for vocational stewardship development suggest that for a fruitful vocational stewardship development journey, Christian educators could not isolate spiritual formation only to the person at a specific age in life. A fruitful vocational stewardship development requires the church to minister to the whole congregation and to embody vocational stewardship in their daily life, social and domestic, and nurture them in their marital and parental roles.

Church Support

While Faith at Work as a social movement has been flourishing among Christians in the United States over the past three decades, David Miller, and many other researchers in this area including Hart and Krueger, Nash and McLennan, and Wuthnow, found that the church's support to help parishioners integrate their faith life and their work life was lacking.[39] Miller summarized his study by saying that "despite some exceptions, the evidence strongly suggests that the church in general seems uninterested in, unaware of, or unsure of how to help laity integrate their faith identities and teachings with their workplace occupations, problems, and possibilities."[40]

---

39. Miller, *God at Work*; see also, Hart and Krueger, "Faith and Work"; Nash and McLennan, *Church on Sunday*; and Wuthnow, *God and Mammon*.

40. Miller, *God at Work*, 81.

Unfortunately, this lack of church support was also experienced by participants in this study. This may suggest that the silence of the church is not
merely a United States problem. The finding is more striking since many
participants are active members in their local churches. Several of them have
even been elders in their churches for quite a number of years. The fact that
a number of participants say that a "church is a place to serve/give, not to
take," even suggests a wider Sunday-Monday gap between the church and
the workplace, and between the clergy and the laity.

Some may suggest that since ecumenical churches have a stronger concern for social engagement such as cultural engagement, poverty, suffering,
human rights, feminist issues, and interfaith issues, that the ecumenical
churches in Indonesia could do better to provide support for their members'
faith and work integration.[41] However, the problem in ecumenical churches,
as Miller suggested of their counterparts in the United States, is the gap
between what the church and clergy did in the macro-level and what the
church members experienced in their weekly church life and daily work
life. As Miller summarized the gap, "The policy papers are largely oriented
to macro-policy and structural questions, usually pertaining to issues of
economic injustice, sustainable development, offshore manufacturing, and
third-world debt forgiveness. However, they seldom speak to the level of
individual vocation, accountability, and responsibility in the marketplace."[42]
He pressed the point further, that "even the statements that attempt to move
to the micro or personal level seldom apply to the average businessperson
or worker in the pew."[43]

The findings of this study seem to be more in accordance with Miller's
observation, instead of the above suggestion. The fact that two-thirds of the
participants this study are members of or affiliated with ecumenical churches
and the rest are members of or affiliated with evangelical churches suggests
that this is the problem of the church in general, regardless of theological
affiliation. Thus, stereotyping between ecumenical and evangelical churches
in Indonesia is not helpful in understanding this situation and coming
to the right solution. If this is the problem of churches in general, more

---

41. Aritonang and Steenbrink, *History of Chritstianity*, 791–803.

42. Miller, *God at Work*, 85.

43. Miller, 85.

intentional effort should be devoted in helping local churches function as an empowering community in the vocational stewardship journey of their members. Related to that, theological schools/seminaries also need to prepare and equip current and future pastors for this task.

Non-Christians in Vocational Stewardship Journey

Following Luther's concept of common grace, recent authors emphasized the importance of seeing the participation of everyone, including non-Christians, to accomplish God's cultural mandate for the common good. Human work is a common vehicle to fulfill that mandate.

As Tim Keller summarized it: "Because all human beings are made in the image of God, and are bestowed with cultural gifts to fulfill their cultural mandate, we should not be surprised that many people without belief in Jesus can do great work – even better work – than Christians."[44]

Living in a religiously diverse context, the contributions of non-Christians are often intertwined with the contributions of Christians as part of the empowering relationship networks for their vocational stewardship journeys. The findings in this study are in accordance with the principle of the common grace. The findings point to the contributions of non-Christian mentors, models, friends, and book authors, in Christian professionals' vocational stewardship development. Besides individual roles, non-faith based communities or communities outside the Christian faith could also become part of empowering communities for vocational stewardship journeys, through shared values, skills storage, or shared concern and support for the common good (e.g. RB; SE; CP; YI; LT).

This reality, in accordance with biblical teaching, suggests a humble attitude for Christian professionals, even in fulfilling the mission to share the foretastes of God's kingdom through their work. Common grace through cultural gifts is a vehicle for God's provision for all humanity. Within this context Christian professionals can benefit from and cooperate with non-Christians. Therefore, in fulfilling God's mission, Hunter suggested a humble attitude that he called "faithful presence." It means "that we are to be fully present to each other within the community of faith and fully present to

---

44. Keller and Alsdorf, *Every Good Endeavor*, 185.

those who are not . . . and direct our lives toward the flourishing of each other through sacrificial love."[45]

Implications for Practice

Based on the insights gained from the discussion of the research findings, a few implications for educational and ministry practices will be explored in this section. Four themes will be highlighted. First, considering insights for spiritual formation in each phase of vocational stewardship development. Second, developing a vocational-stewardship-friendly church. Third, developing a fruitful empowering network for vocational stewardship. These themes will be explored in relation to various contexts for the vocational stewardship development, including the local church, parachurch organizations, and theological schools.

Insights for Spiritual Formation

The research findings provide several key insights to consider in developing a spiritual formation for vocational stewardship development. First, a holistic view of spiritual formation related with multiple dimensions of vocational stewardship. Second, the different phases of vocational stewardship development related to their spiritual and psychosocial development. Third, resources needed for effective spiritual formation related to empowering relationships and empowering communities.

In considering the uniqueness of each vocational stewardship development phase, the suggestion for spiritual formation framework or discipleship strategy will be presented consecutively according to each phase: transformative, transitional, and generative.

Developing a Strong Foundation in the Formative Phase

The formative phase is crucial for the development of vocational stewardship. As the findings suggest, in cases where a few participants did not experience the formation they needed, in their college years or a little afterward, they experienced a prolonged struggle in integrating their faith and work life, or they could not fully "bloom" in their vocational stewardship. On the other

---

45. Hunter, *To Change the World*, 244.

hand, the findings also suggest that a strong foundation in the formative phase provides a solid springboard for further development in the following phases.

A holistic formation

In accordance with literature, the findings suggest the importance of a formation that shapes the whole person including: commitment to follow Christ, biblical framework, values, character, spiritual disciplines, Bible study skills, life skills, and work field exploration. A different perspective has been outlined by several authors (notably Sherman; Dettoni ; and Willard).[46] The cognitive part related with the grammar of vocational stewardship will be addressed separately in the following section.

The findings indicate that, besides cognition, character, spiritual disciplines and some basic skills are vital in their vocational journey. All of these factors need to be nurtured as early as possible to shape the whole aspects of personhood for the task of vocational stewardship. Otherwise, overemphasis only in certain aspects, such as in cognition or activity, will hinder a holistic growth needed for the task.

The grammar of vocational stewardship

The research findings suggest the importance of vocational stewardship grammar both for the vocational journey itself and also as a foundation for ongoing learning. The mastery or fluency in vocational stewardship grammar will enable Christian professionals to have a clear sense of what they are doing in their daily work life from a missional and biblical perspective. It will help them to frame their thoughts in understanding of what is going in the world around them. To understand their context with a critical lens from a biblical perspective, and in what ways can they participate in what God is doing on it.

As a Christian professional entering the generative phase, a mastery or fluency of vocational stewardship grammar will become even more important. In this phase, when suitable learning styles become more experience/problem-centered,[47] a fluency of the grammar would be most helpful. In

---

46. Sherman, *Kingdom Calling*; Dettoni, "Psychology of Adulthood"; Willard, "Spiritual Formation."

47. Knowles, *Modern Practice*.

the generative phase, when their decision making increasingly impacts more people and challenges are more complex due to increasing responsibilities, a mastery of the grammar would also be most helpful. Well informed and biblically based thinking comes from a solid biblical basis and understanding of the context, combined with a well-trained dialectical critical reflection between the text and the context. Therefore, acquiring the grammar of vocational stewardship is crucial for vocational stewardship development in the long run.

Brookfield suggested that the capacity to think critically will normally grow together with the mastery of "the content grammar" and "the epistemological grammar" of the respective subject.[48] In vocational stewardship, "content grammar," could be applied to some relevant basic knowledge such as the theology of work, holistic mission, and public theology. "Epistemological grammar" of vocational stewardship would include critical thinking skills and analysis of daily life issues from multiple lenses such as from biblical, theological, historical, psychological, and sociological perspectives.

What is the relationship between this vocational stewardship grammar and the whole process of learning for vocational stewardship? This simplified outline might be helpful.

    a.   Develop the foundation: basic biblical, theological, and historical knowledge, and basic Bible study skills.

    b.   Develop a basic understanding of vocational stewardship, including a holistic understanding of mission, a biblical understanding of work, and public theology/cultural engagement.

    c.   Develop a basic understanding of a particular profession/field from a biblical perspective, in which the four chapters of the biblical story (Creation, Fall, Redemption, and Consummation) are used as a lens to understand the ideals, challenges, Christ's redemption, and hopes that they can have in their profession/field and their possible participation in the mission of God.

    d.   Develop an ongoing learning process, individually or in a vocation-based group, through the cycle of action-reflection,

---

48. Brookfield, *Teaching for Critical Thinking*, 79–80.

to develop vocational stewardship through their individual and corporate efforts, whether they reflect on strategic/structural or imminent/personal issues.

The first stage (a) should have taken place in the earlier formative phase. The teaching of vocational stewardship grammar (b and c) could be started in the formative phase and consolidated in the transitional phase. If the grammar is well acquired, it will be significantly beneficial for the ongoing learning process (d) that will take place in the long years of the generative phase as Christian professionals face increasing complexities, challenges, and influence in their vocational journey.

Bringing empowering networks closer

The research findings suggest the importance of a model, mentor, or other types of empowering relationships. The findings also suggest that one of the most strategic ways to encourage mentoring relationships to occur is through structuring the relationship by forming small groups that function as a growth group. In this way, both mentoring relationships between the small group leader and members as well as the partnerships among small group members will be facilitated. Further development of the relationships will depend on both the mentor as the group leader and the students as group members. But forming small groups will provide the initial energy to the forming of the empowering relationships.

Models could be part of the faith community, but could also be people of different ages or having a geographical or social distance. Bringing models closer to share their life stories with students will be significantly beneficial. As one participant shared, this kind of practice is helpful for her students. As a professor to her college class, KS also pointed out that this beneficial practice could also be used in other settings:

> I invited guest lecturers for at least one or two subjects. There are practitioners such as [a psychologist] whose area is in industry. Thus, the students can ask, "What kind of struggles does this person have? What are the challenges [he/she faces]? What kind of preparations do I need? What are the things to be considered to be able to survive in such situations?" And since this is related with [faith and work] integration, this

person can explain what it's like for Christian values to be at the workplace . . . I think a good theological foundation is not sufficient, if they cannot see its relationship with how they will work in the future.

The importance of community in the formative phase

The existence of a robust mentoring community is most important in the formative phase. Why is that so? As has been discussed earlier, the task of spiritual formation in this phase is enormous and multidimensional. It involves the shaping of multiple aspects of a person, including the mind (at the "birth of critical consciousness," and in the world flooded with ideas), values and character (that usually would be learned through real-life experiences and sufficient biblical reflection), soft skills (that would be well developed through organizational and leadership experiences), and spiritual disciplines (that need to be developed through practices). Unless the foundational formation has been done earlier, as the findings suggest in one or two rare cases, this means that the whole flock of formative tasks would be crowded into this formative phase.

This background explains why a single mentoring relationship would normally not be sufficient for the formative task. As the research findings suggest, they were helped by models found in the larger community, who embodied vocational stewardship principles. These models inspired and even in some cases caused radical changes in their perspectives. Research findings also suggest that indepth teaching, including Bible expositions and doctrinal teaching, is among the "solid food" that they received from theologically prepared ministers, and is beyond the ability of most mentors, who in campus ministry are often senior students. They claim that these teachings shaped them or in some other cases provided foundations for the next step in their vocational stewardship journey. The findings also indicate that through ministry responsibilities in their campus fellowship group, they also developed various organizational and ministry skills. Lastly, the regular personal devotion, small group meetings, and large group activities they experienced from week to week for four years in college helped to shape the rhythm of activities in their daily life.

For participants who experienced their formative years in a well-run campus ministry (not in a pioneering stage, or in a down period), these all were interconnected aspects that shaped the different aspects of their life while they were in college. In looking at this picture, it will become obvious that only a well-run mentoring community, instead of a single mentoring relationship or an isolated small group, can do this task well. It takes a whole faith community to enable the matrix of transformation to shape and provide a strong foundation for further vocational stewardship development.[49]

In discussing the power of socialization for spiritual formation, Groome provides two helpful insights. First, he contends that "the self is shaped but not determined by society and culture."[50] The result of the formative process will also depend on the self/the person. Second, that "some of our local communities are more faith filled than others."[51] This means that the effectiveness of a local faith community as an agent of transformation will depend on how much vocational stewardship values are embodied within individuals and corporate life of the community. On the other hand, to be effective in the formative task, Christian educators must also help the students to develop from their conventional faith to the individuative-reflective faith through the development of their critical reflection capacity.[52] This is crucial so that they can fulfill their task as the salt and light in their vocational stewardship journey.

Developing Mentoring Relationships in the Transitional Phase

The research findings, in accordance with literature, suggest the importance of mentoring relationships and community in the transitional phase. Two main tasks in this phase, identified in the research findings, are finding the sweet spot of their calling and early phase of integrating their faith and work. Having lived in a schooling system for many years, this is one of the most crucial transitions, in which people ask whether and how their faith can be integrated into the new social context, their workplace. Thus, Christian educators need to seriously consider providing structures that will help new

---

49. Rambo, *Understanding Religious Conversion*.
50. Groome, *Christian Religious Education*, 113.
51. Groome, 125.
52. Fowler, *Stages of Faith*.

Christian professionals to adjust well in their efforts to integrate their faith into their work life, and in most cases also their married life.

As the research findings indicate, developing mentoring relationships through forming small groups for new Christian professionals would be one of most helpful structures that could be developed. Mature Christian professionals who are in the generative phase would fit very well for the choice of mentors. Often they are available in a local faith community, whether local churches or parachurch organizations. What might need to be developed is a structure like a small group, as part of local church or parachurch program. In this way the community will help to facilitate the forming of the relationships, instead of just leaving it to individual's initiative.

The research findings also indicate the benefit of developing a larger fellowship group for new Christian professionals. In this way, teaching specific to their needs, encounters with models, and a larger network of empowering relationships will be available for new Christian professionals. Considering that in the transition phase people usually move to work in a new city or neighborhood, large group meetings could become a nice entry point for new comers. Within the larger fellowship meetings, the formation of small groups could be promoted, and a larger supporting network could be provided.

One important note: research findings also suggest that, for many new Christian professionals, time constraints due to work demands and other types of social activities could potentially prevent many of them from investing as much time as they did during their student life. Therefore, the function of community might not be as powerful as it was in the formative phase.

In college life, many fellowship groups of campus ministries seemed to be most helpful functioning as formative communities due to the physical, social, and ideological encapsulation that occurs more fully with this approach. However, in the transitional phase, the task of helping emerging adults in transitioning into their work life could potentially be done in parachurch organizations (in a form like new graduate ministries) or local churches, especially for larger churches in urban areas.

Providing Mutual Support Resources in the Generative Phase

The research findings suggest that the generative phase, perhaps starting in early or mid-thirties, is usually marked by increasing responsibility at the workplace and in other social contexts (church, society). With this increase of responsibility, also come both opportunities for more strategic impacts and increasing complexities of the challenges. As Parks suggests, in the later phase after emerging adulthood, the need of others continues to exist as resources in navigating through these life challenges.[53] As they passed the transitional changes, Christian professionals also tend to stay long-term in a local church. Therefore, the faith community, whether local churches or parachurch organizations need to see this need and provide empowering support for Christian professionals in this phase.

However, the research findings, in accordance with literature, also suggest that suitable empowering relationships for this phase tends to be mutual, instead of dependent like in the previous phases. In the generative phase Christian professionals experience a shift from dependent relationships (being mentored, looking at models) to mutual relationships (mutual partnerships, including the increasing role of spouse) and generative relationships (mentoring others, become a model). Therefore, to provide effective support for Christian professionals in this phase, suitable learning approaches and supporting communities need to be considered.

Considering the characteristic in this phase, Christian educators might consider these few practical suggestions:

First, developing mutual support groups, with suitable learning approach such as Groome's shared praxis approach, would be most helpful.[54] The group type could vary, including: a vocation-based group based on similarity of profession or a mixture regardless profession. Considering the important role of spouse in vocational stewardship and also the holistic scope of calling that also include marriage/family life, the group could be a group of couples. The number of members should be no more than ten people to encourage and help the discussions and interactions to be more effective. While a body of materials is more homogeneous for mentoring groups in the transitional phase (related with the vocational stewardship grammar and their specific need in that phase), materials of learning would be much more flexible in this phase. In fact, their concern, interest, and problem would set the direction of which material to choose in a certain period of time. Furthermore,

---

53. Parks, *Big Questions*.

54. Groome, *Sharing Faith*.

learning will be blended with the mutual support in relationships and prayer within the group.

Second, since in this phase Christian professionals developing the type of generative relationships, providing more access for ministry responsibilities would be mutually beneficial for them and for the community. Several possibilities could be considered, including: mentoring new Christian professionals, sharing reflections on their vocational stewardship journey in church or parachurch meetings, ministry responsibilities relevant to their vocational gifts. As the research findings suggest, in accordance with literature, active service in faith community, regardless the relevance with their gifts has a positive impact for their own spirituality. Ministry responsibilities relevant with their vocational gifts, including church or parachurch mission projects related with their vocational gifts would be much more impactful.

Developing a Vocational-Stewardship-Friendly Church

A local church, as the most basic and generic form of faith community, has an important role in the vocational stewardship development of its members. However, as the research findings suggest, in accordance with literature, support from local churches is typically still lacking. This indicates that church leaders do not have awareness that the daily work life of the whole church body has a central role in God's mission. Therefore, developing this awareness is one of the most urgent on the priority list.

However, this awareness needs to be followed up further. As has been discussed in the previous section, local churches have an important part to play as empowering communities in various phases of the vocational stewardship preparation and actual journey. Thus, beyond raising awareness, local churches need to integrate support for vocational stewardship development of their members into the fabric of their corporate life. For this purpose, practical insights could be gleaned from authors and church leaders, who have explored and even benefitted from suggested practices.[55]

Miller suggests a helpful framework of five key aspects that need to be developed in local churches to encourage faith and work integration of its members. First is "a ministry of presence and listening" in which pastors

---

55. E.g. Miller, *God at Work*; Sherman, *Kingdom Calling*; Keller and Alsdorf, *Every Good Endeavor*; and Nelson, *Work Matters*.

develop regular visits to their members at their workplace "as regularly and as naturally as they make hospital and home visits."[56] This simple suggestion is so important. Doing this regularly will not only develop the pastor's awareness, but will also help Christian workers to see that daily work life does matter.

Second is "a ministry of public preaching and prayer" in which Sunday liturgy is organized in such a way to "incorporate awareness of and support for faith-and-work issues, including a commissioning service for business people, careful music selection, and lay participation in worship."[57] This is another strategic step to raise awareness. Incorporating work-matters into central rituals will develop and maintain the awareness of the whole congregation in all phases of vocational stewardship development – that work life is an integral part of their Christian life.

Third is "a ministry of teaching" that equips people to understand workplace issues from a biblical perspective.[58] As the findings of this research suggested, various types of teaching contexts and approaches need to be developed in accordance with the need in each phase of vocational stewardship development. Local churches could play important roles in teaching the foundations of spirituality as well as teaching the grammar of vocational stewardship for their members.

Fourth is "a ministry of spiritual integration" in which church members are trained to develop spiritual disciplines such as personal prayer and devotional study in their daily lives.[59] These are two basic spiritual disciplines that develop awareness of God's presence in the daily life. Other types of relevant spiritual disciplines can be developed as well (see Setran and Kiesling's suggestions, for example).

Fifth is "a ministry of gatherings" of business people "to share, reflect, pray, witness, challenge, and encourage one another in the common desire to be faithful and effective in work."[60] Beyond the limit of "business people," that Miller suggested, various types of vocation-based small-group

---

56. Miller, *God at Work*, 146.
57. Miller, 147.
58. Miller, 147.
59. Miller, 148.
60. Miller, 148.

and large-group meetings could be developed for this purpose. In large urban churches with a lot of professionals as their members, the "gatherings" could be based on various specific professional fields.[61]

This framework of practical insights to be incorporated in local churches is promising. Developing these practices will potentially bring an atmosphere that daily work life does matter as an integral, and even a central part, of God's work. However, as we shall see in the following section, the awareness and readiness of pastors are also influenced by what they learned in seminary. Therefore, to address the issue of vocational stewardship resources more comprehensively, we need to see the larger network of the Christian faith community.

Developing a Fruitful Empowering Network

As was briefly discussed earlier, the various types of empowering communities could be seen as a meso-system, a group of various micro-systems that directly influence vocational stewardship development of a Christian professionals. This includes local churches, campus ministries, workplace ministries, and higher education institutions. Behind these directly influential micro-systems, there are a number of institutions that could be classified as their exo-system. These institutions considerably but indirectly influence these Christian professionals through their teaching and policies, including seminary, denominational leadership, and parachurch leadership.

Considering the interconnectedness of these meso-systems and exo-system, for a robust and comprehensive empowering network development, a few practical suggestions need to be taken into consideration.

First is the mobility of participants in navigating through different phases of life. It is very rare to find a person who stays in the same community for his or her life time. Most participants moved geographically from one city or area to another as they move to the next phase of their vocational stewardship development. As one participant described it, the influences of various empowering relationships and communities were "interwoven as a fabric" in her life journey. This means that each type of faith community could play an important role in vocational stewardship development. All faith communities need to share the biblical vision of work and mission.

---

61. See Keller and Alsdorf, *Every Good Endeavor*.

Second is that each community has a unique role to play. For example, family seems to have a significant role in the introductory phase. For those who join campus fellowship groups, campus ministries seem to have a dominant role in the formative phase. Parachurch organizations seem to have important roles in the transitional phase through their ministry to new graduates. However, as the literature suggests, local churches that are ready to minister to young professionals could also have an important role in this phase. But for the longest part of the vocational journey, local churches could take an important role as an empowering community in the generative phase. These all are rough outlines. A closer look might show a lot of overlap. Thus, each faith community needs to learn its context carefully to be able to see what specific role should developed in order to contribute significantly in the process.

Third is the role of Christian universities and colleges. Due to the centrality of the formative phase that takes place in the college years, Christian higher education institutions could play an important role as a mentoring community for the vocational stewardship development of their students. Integrating the grammar of vocational stewardship into its curriculum and providing a mentoring environment to help students find their calling would be strategic for this purpose.[62]

Fourth is that seminaries could play a strategic role as a hub. Due to their strategic position in research and training, seminaries can play several strategic roles in the meso-system of the faith- at-work movement, including integrating the vision and grammar of vocational stewardship into its curriculum, developing research relevant to vocational stewardship issues, and promoting the awareness and teaching of vocational stewardship for pastors and lay leaders.

Strategic efforts to develop a network of resources for vocational stewardship development have been worked out recently. For example, theological educators in the United States that share a similar vision to develop a faith-at-work concern in the seminary education have collaborated through the

---

62. Clydesdale's evaluative research (*Purposeful Graduate*) provides insights on the effectiveness of earlier efforts to integrate exploration of vocation in eighty-eight Christian universities and colleges in the United States.

Oikonomia Network.[63] More than fifteen seminaries joined this network by the year 2016. More recently a network called Made to Flourish Network has been developed for pastors who share a vision to integrate the faith-at-work concern in their church lives.[64]

A strategic effort that has tried to gather active participants and leaders in various sectors of the faith-at-work movement has been attempted through a working conference called Faith@Work Summit, held for the first time in 2014 in Boston, followed in 2016 in Dallas, and in 2018 in Chicago. Five key sectors were included in the Faith@Work Summit 2016: global business arena, universities and business schools, seminaries and bible schools, the church, and workplace ministry organizations.[65] These networks are promising since they encourage a more comprehensive vision and the spirit of collaboration for all stakeholders in participating in God's work to bring the foretaste of his shalom and Christ's transforming power through workplaces around the world.

Suggestions for Further Research

This study focused on the development of vocational stewardship among Indonesian Christian professionals. The research findings contributed educational insights to the literature on the theology of work and faith-at-work movement. This study delimited its scope to a qualitative research among Christian professionals with the majority of participants having campus ministry background. However, this study also opened the way for further inquiries in multiple directions.

First, a broader pool of respondents with multiple backgrounds will provide a more comprehensive picture of vocational stewardship development among Indonesian Christian professionals, based on a qualitative research. This includes a significant number of participants without campus ministry background.

Second, a quantitative research to see the ability to generalize the findings in the Indonesian context. This will provide a wider scope of observation

---

63. See http://oikonomianetwork.org/about/ for more information.
64. See https://www.madetoflourish.org/about/ for more information.
65. See http://fwsummit.org/ for more information.

coverage compared to the limited number of respondents in a qualitative study. At the same time the data gathered from this quantitative study will also complement the data gathered from the qualitative study.

Third, research to see how Christian educators, including pastors, campus ministers and seminary professors in Indonesia perceive the connection between non-clergy's work and God's work, and what they do or think they need to do to help their church members for that purpose. Since their role is strategic in the development of vocational stewardship of Christian professionals and Christian workers in general, the result would provide important insights for practice.

Conclusion

This research offered insights for spiritual formation focusing on the development of vocational stewardship in Christian professionals. The research findings suggest four consecutive phases of the development: introductory, formative, transitional, and generative. Each phase has its own characteristics, which to certain extent are influenced by the relevant developmental stage: childhood and adolescence, early part of emerging adulthood, later part of emerging adulthood, and tested adulthood, followed by mature adulthood.[66]

Without necessarily undermining other phases, the formative phase is central for a promising vocational stewardship development. For the majority of participants in this study, this phase occurred in the early part of their emerging adulthood, during their college years. A formation that provides a solid foundation for the whole personhood is crucial for a robust vocational stewardship development in the following phases. The transitional phase, occurring in the later part of emerging adulthood, in the first few post-college years, also needs special attention from Christian educators and ministers. Among others, Christian educators and ministers would be most helpful in this phase by helping those in these two phases to learn "the grammar" of vocational stewardship, structuring empowering relationships through small groups, and bringing models closer to their daily lives. A faith community

---

66. Parks, *Big Questions*.

that fully functions as a matrix of transformation (Rambo 1993) would be most helpful in the formative phase.[67]

The development of vocational stewardship in the generative phase, in adulthood, is quite different from the previous phases. Christian educators and ministers must take into consideration the shift from a dependent to a mutual type of learning and support more suitable for this phase. In this phase the role of spouse and faith community appeared to be strong. Workplace ministry and active service in faith communities is indirectly beneficial to participants. However, local churches need to provide more intentional support for their congregations. Unlike the tendency for short-term participation in the previous two phases, having more settled residentially, in this phase people tend to stay long-term in a local church. In general, the data suggest that local churches need to work hard to develop a vocational-stewardship-friendly church to intentionally support the development of vocational stewardship for their members.

Lastly, the findings suggest that the development of vocational stewardship in each phase is strongly influenced by various types of empowering communities. Since these communities are interrelated with each other like an ecological system,[68] to develop a fruitful support for vocational stewardship developments, Christian leaders need to address this concern in multiple spheres, including local churches, campus ministry, workplace ministry, Christian colleges and universities, and seminaries.

---

67. Rambo, *Understanding Religious Conversion*.
68. Bronfenbrenner, *Ecology of Human*.

APPENDIX 1

Informed Consent Form

Thank you for your willingness to participate in this study. Your contribution in this study is highly appreciated.

The research in which you are about to participate is designed to investigate the personal development of vocational stewardship among Indonesian Christian professionals. This research is being conducted by Sutrisna Harjanto, a PhD student in the Educational Studies program at Trinity Evangelical Divinity School. In this research you will be asked to share your life stories pertinent with the topic. Your response will be recorded for further analysis for the purpose of this study. Upon completion of the study, your recorded responses will be deleted.

Please be assured that the researcher will take extensive measures to protect your anonymity and honor confidentiality. At no time will your name be reported along with your responses. Please understand that your participation in this research is totally voluntary and you are free to withdraw at any time during this study.

"I acknowledge that I have been informed of, and understand, the nature and purpose of this study, and I freely consent to participate."

Name _____

Signed _____ Date_____

APPENDIX 2

Interview Questions

RQ-1. How do Indonesian Christian professionals describe their vocational stewardship?

   1.1. Can you give a brief description of what kind of work that you have been doing so far?

   1.2. Can you recall circumstances or considerations that have led you to choose to work at this field/company/geographical area?

   1.3. Please describe how your faith has influenced your work life (principles, attitude, etc.)

   1.4. How do you describe the connection between your work and God's work, if there is any?

RQ-2. How do Indonesian Christian professionals describe the significance of their college years for the development of their vocational stewardship?

   2.1. In what ways have your college years contributed to your understanding and attitude in your work life? (OR for participants without campus ministry background: In what ways have your early twenties contributed to your understanding and attitude in your work life?)

   2.2. Can you recall any influences that lead you to awareness that your work is important for God's mission? How have these experiences affected your work life?

2.3.   Think of some persons (mentor, pastor, professor, friend, family, etc.) or communities in your college years which have been significantly helpful for you in developing the connection between your work and God's work. In what ways (if there are) have they been helpful?

RQ-3.   How do Indonesian Christian professionals describe the personal development of vocational stewardship after their college years?

3.1.   In what ways have your post-college years contributed to your understanding and attitude in your work life?

3.2.   Think of some persons (mentor, pastor, friend, family, etc.) or communities in your life journey after your college years which have been significantly helpful to develop the connection between your work and God's work. In what ways have they been helpful?

3.3.   If you are asked to help another Christian professional to connect his/her work with God's work, what are some of the things that you would offer?

Bibliography

Aritonang, Jan S., and Karel A. Steenbrink, eds. *A History of Christianity in Indonesia*. Studies in Christian Mission, volume 35. Leiden: Brill, 2008.

Arnett, Jeffrey J. *Adolescence and Emerging Adulthood: A Cultural Approach*. 5th edition. Boston, MA: Pearson, 2013.

———. *Emerging Adulthood: The Winding Road from the Late Teens through the Twenties*. Oxford: Oxford University Press, 2006.

———. *Emerging Adulthood: The Winding Road from the Late Teens through the Twenties*. 2nd edition. New York: Oxford University Press, 2015.

———. "Emerging Adulthood: A Theory of Development from the Late Teens through the Twenties." *American Psychologist* 55, no. 5 (May 2000): 469–480.

Atkinson, Harley. "Annotated Bibliography for the Use of Small Groups in Contemporary Christian Formation." *Christian Educational Journal* 11, no. 1 (2014): 166–172.

Bakke, Dennis. *Joy at Work: A Revolutionary Approach to Fun on the Job*. Seattle, WA: PVG, 2005.

Balswick, Jack O., Pamela E. King, and Kevin S. Reimer. *The Reciprocating Self: Human Development in Theological Perspective*. 2nd edition. Downers Grove, IL: InterVarsity, 2016.

Banks, Robert J. *God the Worker: Journeys into the Mind, Heart and Imagination of God*. Eugene, OR: Wipf & Stock, 2008.

Baucum, Tory. *Evangelical Hospitality: Catechical Evangelism in the Early Church and Its Recovery for Today*. Lanham, MD: Scarecrow Press, 2008.

Berger, Peter L. *The Sacred Canopy*. Garden City, NY: Doubleday; Anchor Books, 1969.

Berger, Peter L., and Thomas Luckmann. *The Social Construction of Reality*. Garden City, NY: Doubleday, 1966.

Bolt, John. *Economic Shalom: A Reformed Primer on Faith, Work, and Human Flourishing*. Grand Rapids, MI: Christian's Library Press, 2013.

Boren, Scott, and Jim Egli. "Small Group Models: Navigating the Commonalities and the Differences." *Christian Educational Journal* 11, no. 1 (2014): 152–165.

Bosch, David Jacobus. *Transforming Mission: Paradigm Shifts in Theology of Mission.* Maryknoll, NY: Orbis Books, 1991.

BPS Indonesia. "Proyeksi Penduduk menurut Provinsi, 2010–2035." Badan Pusat Statistik Indonesia, 2014. Accessed 17 October 2016 http://www.bps.go.id/linkTabelStatis/view/id/1274.

———. "Sensus Penduduk 2010: Penduduk Menurut Kelompok Umur and Agama yang Dianut." Badan Pusat Statistik Indonesia, 2010. Accessed 17 October 2016 http://sp2010.bps.go.id/index.php/site/tabel?tid=320danwid=0.

———. "Sensus Penduduk 2010: Penduduk Menurut Wilayah and Agama yang Dianut." Badan Pusat Statistik Indonesia, 2010. Accessed 17 October 2016 http://sp2010.bps.go.id/index.php/site/tabel?search-tabel=Penduduk+Menurut+Wilayah+dan+Agama+yang+Dianutdantid=321dansearch-wilayah=Indonesiadanwid=0000000000danlang=id.

———. "Sensus Penduduk 2010: Pendidikan yang Ditamatkan." Badan Pusat Statistik Indonesia, 2010. Accessed 17 October 2016 http://sp2010.bps.go.id/index.php/site/topik?kid=6dankategori=Pendidikan.

Brand, Chad. *Flourishing Faith: A Baptist Primer on Work, Economics, and Civic Stewardship.* Grand Rapids, MI: Christian's Library Press, 2013.

Bronfenbrenner, U. *The Ecology of Human Development: Experiments by Nature and Design.* Cambridge, MA: Harvard University Press, 1979.

Brookfield, Stephen. *Developing Critical Thinkers: Challenging Adults to Explore Alternative Ways of Thinking and Acting.* 1st edition. San Francisco, CA: Jossey-Bass, 1987.

———. *Teaching for Critical Thinking: Tools and Techniques to Help Students Question Their Assumptions.* 1st edition. San Francisco, CA: Jossey-Bass, 2012.

———. *Understanding and Facilitating Adult Learning.* San Francisco, CA: Jossey-Bass, 1986.

Browne, LaVonne A. 1972-(LaVonne Antoinette). "On Faith and Work: The Relationship between Religiosity and Work Values." Dissertation from the University of Missouri-Columbia, 2001.

Buechner, Frederick. *Wishful Thinking: A Seeker's ABC.* New York, NY: HarperOne, 1993.

Burkey, Julie V. "Theology of Work: A Working Life Retreat." Dissertation from the Catholic University of America, 2011.

Clydesdale, Tim. *The Purposeful Graduate: Why Colleges Must Talk to Students about Vocation.* Chicago, IL: University of Chicago Press, 2015.

Cosden, Darrell. *The Heavenly Good of Earthly Work*. Milton Keynes, UK: Paternoster Press, 2006.

———. *A Theology of Work: Work and the New Creation*. Eugene, OR: Wipf & Stock, 2006. (First published by Paternoster, 2004)

Costas, Orlando E. *Christ Outside the Gate: Mission Beyond Christendom*. Eugene, OR: Wipf & Stock, 2005. (First published by Orbis, 1982)

———. *The Church and Its Mission: A Shattering Critique from the Third World*. Wheaton, IL: Tyndale House, 1974.

———. *The Integrity of Mission: The Inner Life and Outreach of the Church*. San Francisco, CA: Harper & Row, 1979.

Cote, James. "The Dangerous Myth of Emerging Adulthood: An Evidenced-Based Critique of a Flawed Developmental Theory." *Applied Developmental Science* 18, no. 4 (2014): 177–188.

Côté, James, and John M. Bynner. "Changes in the Transition to Adulthood in the UK and Canada: The Role of Structure and Agency in Emerging Adulthood." *Journal of Youth Studies* 11, no. 3 (2008): 251–268.

Cranton, Patricia. *Understanding and Promoting Transformative Learning: A Guide for Educators of Adults*. 2nd edition. San Francisco, CA: Jossey-Bass, 2006.

Creswell, John W. *Educational Research: Planning, Conducting, and Evaluating Quantitative and Qualitative Research*. 4th edition. Boston, MA: Pearson, 2012.

Crouch, Andy. *Culture Making: Recovering Our Creative Calling*. Downers Grove, IL: InterVarsity, 2008.

Davis, John Jefferson. "Will There Be New Work in the New Creation?" *Evangelical Review of Theology* 31, no. 3 (2007): 256–273.

Dettoni, John M. "Psychology of Adulthood." In *The Christian Educator's Handbook on Adult Education*, edited by Kenneth O. Gangel and James C. Wilhoit, 77–90. Wheaton, IL: Victor Books, 1993.

Dewey, John. *Experience and Education*. New York: Touchstone, 1938.

Donahue, Bill, and Charles Gowler. "Small Groups: The Same Today, Yesterday, and Forever?" *Christian Educational Journal* 11, no. 1 (2014): 118–133.

Downs, P. *Teaching for Spiritual Growth: An Introduction to Christian Education*. Grand Rapids, MI: Zondervan, 1994.

Dunn, Richard R., and Jana L. Sundene. *Shaping the Journey of Emerging Adults: Life-Giving Rhythms for Spiritual Transformation*. Downers Grove, IL: InterVarsity, 2012.

Dyrness, William A. *Let the Earth Rejoice!: A Biblical Theology of Holistic Mission*. Westchester, IL: Crossway, 1983.

End, Van Den. *Harta Dalam Bejana: Sejarah Gereja Ringkas*. Jakarta: BPK Gunung Mulia, 1999.

———. *Ragi Carita 1, Sejarah Gereja di Indonesia 1500 – 1860.* Jakarta: BPK Gunung Mulia, 1999.

———. *Ragi Carita 2, Sejarah Gereja di Indonesia 1860 – Sekarang.* Jakarta: BPK Gunung Mulia, 1999.

Erikson, Erik H. *Childhood and Society.* 2nd edition. New York: W. W. Norton, 1963.

———. *The Life Cycle Completed.* New York: W. W. Norton, 1998.

Escobar, Samuel. *Christian Mission and Social Justice.* Scottdale, PA: Herald Press, 1978.

Estep Jr., James R. "Moral Development and Christian Formation." In *Christian Formation: Integrating Theology and Human Development,* edited by James R. Estep Jr. and Jonathan H. Kim, 123–160. Nashville, TN: B & H Academic, 2010.

Fletcher, C. M. "Restoring the Sense of Divine Vocation to Work: A Study of Sayers, MacIntyre and Catholic Social Teaching." Dissertation. CNAA, Anglia Polytechnic, UK, 2006.

Fowler, James W. *Stages of Faith: The Psychology of Human Development and the Quest for Meaning.* New York: Harper & Row, 1981.

Fowler, James W., K. Nipkow, and F. Schweitzer, eds. *Stages of Faith and Religious Development: Implications for Church, Education, and Society.* New York: Crossroad, 1991.

Freire, Paulo. "Education as the Practice of Freedom." In *Education for Critical Consciousness,* translated and edited by Myra B. Ramos, 1–80. New York: Continuum, 2008[1967].

———. *Pedagogy of the Oppressed.* New York: Seabury Press, 1973[1970].

Fry, Louis W., and David Geigle. "Spirituality and Religion in the Workplace: History, Theory, and Research." *Psychology of Religion and Spirituality* 6, no. 3 (2014): 175–187.

Garber, Steven. *The Fabric of Faithfulness: Weaving Together Belief and Behavior.* Expanded edition. Downers Grove, IL: InterVarsity, 2007.

———. *Visions of Vocation: Common Grace for the Common Good.* Downers Grove, IL: InterVarsity, 2014.

Gilligan, Carol. *In A Different Voice: Psychological Theory and Women's Development.* Cambridge, MA: Harvard University Press, 1982.

Greenman, Jeffrey P. "Spiritual Formation in Theological Perspective: Classic Issues, Contemporary Challenges." In *Life in the Spirit: Spiritual Formation in Theological Perspective,* edited by Jeffrey P. Greenman and George Kalantzis, 23–35. Downers Grove, IL: InterVarsity, 2010.

Groome, Thomas H. *Christian Religious Education: Sharing Our Story and Vision.* San Francisco, CA: Harper & Row, 1980.

————. *Sharing Faith: A Comprehensive Approach to Religious Education and Pastoral Ministry: The Way of Shared Praxis*. San Francisco, CA: Harper, 1991.

Guinness, Os. *The Call: Finding and Fulfilling the Central Purpose of Your Life*. Nashville, TN: Word, 1998.

Hamant, William R. "A Pioneer in Roman Catholic Social Thought: The Anthropology and Theology of Work of Bishop Wilhelm Emmanuel Freiherrn von Ketteler," 2001.

Hammond, Pete, Paul Stevens, and Todd Svanoe. *The Marketplace Annotated Bibliography: A Christian Guide to Books on Work, Business and Vocation*. Downers Grove, IL: InterVarsity, 2002.

Hardy, Lee. *The Fabric of This World: Inquiries into Calling, Career Choice, and the Design of Human Work*. Grand Rapids, MI: Eerdmans, 1990.

————. "Review of Work in the Spirit: Toward a Theology of Work." *Calvin Theological Journal* 28, no. 1 (1993): 191–196.

Hart, Stephen, and David A. Krueger. "Faith and Work: Challenges for Congregations." *Christian Century* (July 1992): 683–686.

Haughey, John C. *Converting Nine to Five: Bringing Spirituality to Your Daily Work*. Eugene, OR: Wipf & Stock, 2005.

Hendry, Leo B., and Marion Kloep. "Conceptualizing Emerging Adulthood: Inspecting the Emperor's New Clothes?" In *Taking Sides: Clashing Views in Lifespan Development*, edited by Andrew M. Guest, 281–287. Boston, MA: McGraw Hill, 2009.

Hesselgrave, David J. *Paradigms in Conflict: 10 Key Questions in Christian Missions Today*. Grand Rapids, MI: Kregel, 2005.

————. "Redefining Holism." *Evangelical Missions Quarterly* 35 (July 1999): 278–284.

Horell, Harold D. "Thomas Groome." Talbot School of Theology, Biola University, 2016. Accessed 16 November 2016 http://www.talbot.edu/ce20/educators/catholic/thomas_groome/.

Hunter, James. *To Change the World: The Irony, Tragedy, and Possibility of Christianity in the Late Modern World*. Oxford: Oxford University Press, 2010.

Jensen, David Hadley. *Responsive Labor: A Theology of Work*. Louisville, KY: Westminster John Knox Press, 2006.

Johnson, Neal, and Steve Rundle. "Business as Mission: From Impoverished to Empowered." In *Evangelical Missiological Society*, series no. 14, edited by Tom A. Steffen and Mike Barnett, 19–36. Pasadena, CA: William Carey Library,2009.

Johnson, C. Neal. *Business as Mission: A Comprehensive Guide to Theory and Practice*. Downers Grove, IL: IVP Academic, 2009.

Jolley, A. J. "Bridging the Gap: How Christians Can Relate Their Faith and Their Work." Dissertation from the University of Nottingham, 2006.

Jorgensen, Gunnar. "Kohlberg and Gilligan: Duet or Duel?" *Journal of Moral Education* 35, no. 2 (1 June 2006): 179–196.

Kegan, Robert. *The Evolving Self: Problem and Process in Human Development.* Cambridge, MA: Harvard University Press, 1982.

———. *In Over Our Heads: The Mental Demands of Modern Life.* Cambridge, MA: Harvard University Press, 1994.

———. "There the Dance Is: Religious Dimensions of a Developmental Framework." In *Toward Moral and Religious Maturity*, edited by Christiane Brusselmans. Morristown, NJ: Silver Burdett, 1981.

Kegan, Robert, and Lisa L. Lahey. *Immunity to Change: How to Overcome It and Unlock the Potential in Yourself and Your Organization.* Boston: Harvard Business Press, 2009.

Keller, Timothy J. *Generous Justice: How God's Grace Makes Us Just.* New York: Dutton, 2010.

Keller, Timothy J., and Katherine Alsdorf. *Every Good Endeavor: Connecting Your Work to God's Work.* New York: Dutton, 2012.

Knapp, John C. "Bridging Christian Ethics and Economic Life: Where Pastors and Laity Disconnect." *Journal for Preachers* 28, no. 2 (2005): 47–54.

Knoema. "Number of Students in Tertiary Education per 100,000 Inhabitants." UNESCO Institute for Statistics Data, 2013. Accessed 17 October 2016. https://knoema.com/UNESCOISD2013Jul/unesco-institute-for-statistics-data-2013?location=1000920-indonesia.

Knowles, Malcolm S. "Contribution of Malcolm Knowles." In *The Christian Educator's Handbook on Adult Education*, edited by Kenneth O. Gangel and James C. Wilhoit, 91–103. Wheaton, IL: Victor Books, 1993.

———. *The Modern Practice of Adult Education: From Pedagogy to Andragogy.* Chicago, IL: Follett, 1980.

Knowles, Malcolm S., Elwood F. Holton, and Richard A. Swanson. *The Adult Learner: The Definitive Classic in Adult Education and Human Resource Development.* 7th edition. London: Routledge, 2012.

Kuhmerker, Lisa. *The Kohlberg Legacy for the Helping Professions.* Birmingham: R.E.P. Books, 1991.

Labouvie-Vief, G. "Emerging Structures of Adult Thought." In *Emerging Adults in America: Coming of Age in the 21st Century*, edited by J. J. Arnett and J. Tanner, 59–84. Washington, DC: American Psychological Association, 2006.

Langer, Richard. "Niggle's Leaf and Holland's Opus: Reflections on the Theological Significance of Work." *Evangelical Review of Theology* 33, no. 2 (2009): 100–117.

Larive, Armand. *After Sunday: A Theology of Work*. New York: Continuum, 2004.

Lausanne Movement. "The Cape Town Commitment." Lausanne Movement, 2010. Accessed 11 November 2016. https://www.lausanne.org/content/ctc/ctcommitment.

———. "The Lausanne Covenant." Lausanne Movement, 1974. http://www.lausanne.org/en/component/content/article.html?id=26.

Liu, Timothy, Gordon Preece, and Siew Li Wong. "Marketplace Ministry: Occasional Paper No. 40." Lausanne Committee for World Evangelization, 2004. Accessed 11 November 2016. https://www.lausanne.org/wp-content/uploads/2007/06/LOP40_IG11.pdf.

McGavran, Donald A. *Understanding Church Growth*. Grand Rapids, MI: Eerdmans, 1970.

MacKeracher, Dorothy. *Making Sense of Adult Learning*. Toronto: University of Toronto Press, 2004.

Marques, Joan, Satinder Dhiman, and Richard King. *The Workplace and Spirituality: New Perspectives on Research and Practice*. Woodstock, VT: Skylight Paths, 2009.

Marshall, Paul A., and Lela Gilbert. *Heaven Is Not My Home: Learning to Live in God's Creation*. Nashville, TN: Word Pub, 1998.

Marshall, Rich. *God @ Work: Discovering the Anointing for Business*. Shippensburg, PA: Destiny Image Publishers, 2000.

Merriam, Sharan B. *Qualitative Research: A Guide to Design and Implementation*. San Francisco, CA: Jossey-Bass, 2009.

Merriam, Sharan B., and Laura L. Bierema. *Adult Learning: Linking Theory and Practice*. San Francisco, CA: Jossey-Bass, 2014.

Merriam, Sharan B., Rosemary S. Caffarella, and Lisa M. Baumgartner. *Learning in Adulthood: A Comprehensive Guide*. 3rd edition. San Francisco, CA: John Wiley & Sons, 2007.

Mezirow, Jack. *Education for Perspective Transformation: Women's Re-Entry Programs in Community Colleges*. New York: Center for Adult Education, Teachers College, Columbia University, 1978.

———. *Learning as Transformation: Critical Perspectives on a Theory in Progress*. San Francisco, CA: Jossey-Bass, 2000.

Miller, David W. *God at Work: The History and Promise of the Faith at Work Movement*. Oxford: Oxford University Press, 2007.

Moberg, David. *The Great Reversal: Evangelism versus Social Concern*. Philadelphia, PA: J. B. Lippincott, 1972.

Morgan, David L. *Focus Group as Qualitative Research*. 2nd edition. Qualitative Research Methods Series 16. Thousand Oaks, CA: Sage, 1997.

Nash, Laura L., and Scotty McLennan. *Church on Sunday, Work on Monday: The Challenge of Fusing Christian Values with Business Life*. San Francisco, CA: Jossey-Bass, 2001.

Neal, Judi. *Handbook of Faith and Spirituality in the Workplace: Emerging Research and Practice*. Fayetteville, AR: Springer, 2013.

Nelson, Tom. *Work Matters: Connecting Sunday Worship to Monday Work*. Wheaton, IL: Crossway, 2011.

Newman, Las. "Foreword." In *Holistic Mission: God's Plan for God's People*, edited by Brian Woolnough and Wonsuk Ma, ix–x. Oxford: Regnum, 2010.

Niebuhr, H. Richard. *Christ and Culture*. New York: Harper & Row, 1951.

Ott, Craig, and Stephen J. Strauss. *Encountering Theology of Mission Biblical Foundations, Historical Developments, and Contemporary Issues*. Grand Rapids, MI: Baker Academic, 2010.

Padilla, C. René. *Mission Between the Times: Essays*. Grand Rapids, MI: Eerdmans, 1985.

———. "Holistic Mission." In *Dictionary of Mission Theology*, edited by John Corrie. Downers Grove, IL: InterVarsity, 2007.

Parks, Sharon Daloz. *Big Questions, Worthy Dreams: Mentoring Emerging Adults in Their Search for Meaning, Purpose, and Faith*. Revised edition. San Francisco, CA: Jossey-Bass, 2011.

Parrett, Gary A., and Steve Kang. *Teaching the Faith, Forming the Faithful: A Biblical Vision for Education in the Church*. Downers Grove, IL: InterVarsity, 2009.

Patton, Michael Quinn. *Qualitative Research and Evaluation Methods*. 3rd edition. Thousand Oaks, CA: Sage, 2002.

Pascarella, E., and P. Terenzini. *How College Affects Students: Findings and Insights from Twenty Years of Research*. San Francisco, CA: Jossey-Bass, 1991.

Perkins, William. "A Treatise of the Vocations." In *Callings: Twenty Centuries of Christian Wisdom on Vocation*, edited by William C. Placher, 262–272. Grand Rapids, MI: Eerdmans, 2005.

Perricone, John A. "Catholic Theology of Work and Worship." *St. John's Law Review* 73, no. 1 (Winter 1999): 821–203.

Perry, William Graves. *Forms of Intellectual and Ethical Development in the College Years: A Scheme*. New York: Holt, Rinehart & Winston, 1970.

Peskett, Howard, and Vinoth Ramachandra. *The Message of Mission: The Glory of Christ in All Time and Space*. Downers Grove, IL: InterVarsity, 2003.

Peters, R. S. *The Philosophy of Education*. London: Oxford University Press, 1973.

Piaget, Jean. *The Psychology of Intelligence*. Totowa, NJ: Littlefield, Adams & Co., 1966.

Placher, William C., ed. *Callings: Twenty Centuries of Christian Wisdom on Vocation*. Grand Rapids, MI: Eerdmans, 2005.

Pope John Paul II. "Laborem Exercens: Encyclical Letter." 1981. Accessed 6 November 2014. http://www.catholic-pages.com/documents/laborem_exercens.pdf.

Prior, John M., and Alle Hoekema. "Theological Thinking by Indonesian Christians 1850–2000." In *A History of Christianity in Indonesia,* edited by Jan Sihar Aritonang and Karel Steenbrink, 749–821. Leiden: Brill, 2008.

Rambo, Lewis. *Understanding Religious Conversion.* New Haven, CO: Yale University Press, 1993.

Rifkin, Jeremy. *The End of Work: The Decline of the Global Labor Force and the Dawn of the Post-Market Era.* New York: G. P. Putnam's Sons, 1995.

Rundle, Steve. "Restoring the Role of Business in Mission." In *Perspectives on the World Christian Movement: A Reader*, edited by Ralph D. Winter and Steven C. Hawthorne, 757–763. Pasadena, CA: William Carey Library, 2009.

Ryken, Leland. *Work and Leisure in Christian Perspective.* Portland, OR: Multnomah Press, 1987.

Sasongko, Grace, Philip Ayus, Sutrisna Harjanto, and Yulius Tandyanto. *Kisah yang Belum Usai: Menyibak Karya Ilahi Melalui Dunia Kampus.* Jakarta: Literatur Perkantas, 2011.

Schumacer, Christian. *God at Work: Discovering the Divine Pattern for Work in the New Millenium.* Oxford: Lion, 1998.

Schuurman, Douglas James. *Vocation: Discerning Our Callings in Life.* Grand Rapids, MI: Eerdmans, 2004.

Seidman, Irving. *Interviewing as Qualitative Research: A Guide for Researchers in Education and the Social Sciences.* New York: Teachers College Press, 2013.

Self, Charlie. *Flourishing Churches and Communities: A Pentecostal Primer on Faith, Work, and Economics for Spirit-Empowered Discipleship.* Grand Rapids, MI: Christian's Library Press, 2012.

Setran, David P., and Chris A. Kiesling. *Spiritual Formation in Emerging Adulthood: A Practical Theology for College and Young Adult Ministry.* Grand Rapids, MI: Baker Academic, 2013.

Sherblom, Stephen. "The Legacy of the 'Care Challenge': Re-Envisioning the Outcome of the Justice-Care Debate." *Journal of Moral Education* 37, no. 1 (March 2008): 81–98.

Sherman, Amy L. *Kingdom Calling: Vocational Stewardship for the Common Good.* Downers Grove, IL: InterVarsity, 2011.

Sherman, Doug, and William Hendricks. *Your Work Matters to God.* Colorado Springs, CO: NavPress, 1990.

Silva, J. M. "Constructing Adulthood in an Age of Uncertainty." *American Sociological Review* 77 (2012): 505–522.

Sinnott, J. D. "Postformal Thought and Adult Development: Living in Balance." In *Handbook of Adult Development*, edited by J. Demick and C. Andreoti, 221–238. New York: Kluwer, 2003.

Sousa, David A. *How the Brain Learns*. 4th edition. Thousand Oaks, CA: Corwin, 2011.

Stanley, Paul, and J. Robert Clinton. *Connecting: The Mentoring Relationships You Need to Succeed in Life*. Colorado Spring, CO: NavPress, 1992.

Stevens, R. Paul. *Doing God's Business: Meaning and Motivation for the Marketplace*. Grand Rapids, MI: Eerdmans, 2006.

———. *Work Matters: Lessons from Scripture*. Grand Rapids, MI: Eerdmans, 2012.

Stonehouse, Catherine. "The Power of Kohlberg." In *Nurture That Is Christian*, edited by James C. Wilhoit and John M. Dettoni, 61–74. Grand Rapids, MI: Baker Books, 1998.

Stott, John. *The Contemporary Christian: Applying God's World to Today's World*. Downers Grove, IL: InterVarsity, 1992.

———. *Issues Facing Christians Today*. 4th edition, fully revised. and updated. Grand Rapids, MI: Zondervan, 2006.

Taylor, Edward W., and Patricia Cranton. "Transformative Learning Theory: Seeking a More Unified Theory." In *The Handbook of Transformative Learning: Theory, Research, and Practice*, edited by Edward W. Taylor, and Patricia Cranton, 3–20. San Francisco, CA: Jossey-Bass, 2012.

Terkel, Studs. *Working: People Talk about What They Do All Day and How They Feel about What They Do*. New York: New Press, 1974.

Tizon, Al. "Precursors and Tensions in Holistic Mission: An Historical Overview." In *Holistic Mission: God's Plan for God's People*, edited by Brian E. Woolnough and Wonsuk Ma, 61–75. Oxford: Regnum, 2010.

Tunehag, Mats, Wayne McGee, and Josie Plummer. "Business as Mission: Lausanne Occasional Paper No. 59." Lausanne Committee for World Evangelization, 2005. Accessed 11 November 2016. https://www.lausanne.org/docs/2004forum/LOP59_IG30.pdf.

Transparency International. *Corruption by Country/Territory: Indonesia*. 2016. Accessed 17 October 2016. http://www.transparency.org/country#IDN.

Vallas, Steven P., William Finlay, and Amy S. Wharton. *The Sociology of Work: Structure and Inequalities*. New York: Oxford University Press, 2009.

Van Duzer, Jeffrey B. *Why Business Matters to God: And What Still Needs to Be Fixed*. Downers Grove, IL: InterVarsity, 2010.

Volf, Miroslav. "Eschaton, Creation, and Social Ethics." *Calvin Theological Journal* 30, no. 1 (1995): 130–143.

———. *Work in the Spirit: Toward a Theology of Work*. Oxford: Oxford University Press, 1991.

WCC. "Resource Book: World Council of Churches 10th Assembly."
World Council of Churches Publications, 2013. Accessed 13 December
2015. http://wcc2013.info/en/resources/documents/ResourceBook_en.pdf.

Wilhoit, Jim, and John M. Dettoni, eds. *Nurture That Is Christian: Developmental
Perspectives on Christian Education*. Wheaton, IL: Victor Books, 1995.

Willard, Dallas. "Spiritual Formation in Christ Is for the Whole Life and the
Whole Person." In *For All The Saints: Evangelical Theology and Christian
Spirituality*, edited by Timothy George and Alister McGrath, 39–54.
Louisville, KY: Westminster John Knox Press, 2003.

Witherington III, Ben. *Work: A Kingdom Perspective on Labor*. Grand Rapids,
MI: Eerdmans, 2011.

Wolters, Albert M. *Creation Regained: Biblical Basics for a Reformational
Worldview*. 2nd edition. Grand Rapids, MI: Eerdmans, 2005.

Wood, Ralph C. "Outward Faith, Inward Piety: The Dependence of Spirituality
on Worship and Doctrine." In *For all the Saints: Evangelical Theology and
Christian Spirituality*, edited by Timothy George and Alister McGrath,
91–108. Louisville, KY: Westminster John Knox Press, 2003.

Woolnough, Brian E., and Wonsuk Ma, eds. *Holistic Mission: God's Plan for God's
People*. Oxford: Regnum, 2010.

World Bank. "Indonesia: Rising Inequality Risks Long-Term Growth
Slowdown." The World Bank, 2015. Accessed 17 October 2016. http://
www.worldbank.org/en/news/press-release/2015/12/08/rising-inequality-
risks-long-term-growth-slowdown.

Wright, Christopher J. H. T*he Mission of God's People: A Biblical Theology of the
Church's Mission*. Grand Rapids, MI: Zondervan, 2010.

———. *The Mission of God: Unlocking the Bible's Grand Narrative*. Downers
Grove, IL: InterVarsity, 2006.

Wright, David. *How God Makes the World a Better Place: A Wesleyan Primer on
Faith, Work, and Economic Transformation*. Grand Rapids, MI: Christian's
Library Press, 2012.

Wright, N. T. "Righteousness." In *New Dictionary of Theology*, edited by David F.
Wright, Sinclair B. Ferguson, and J. I. Packer, 590–592. Downers Grove, IL:
InterVarsity, 1988.

Wuthnow, Robert. *God and Mammon in America*. New York: Macmillan, 1994.

Wyszyński, Stefan. *All You Who Labor: Work and the Sanctification of Daily Life*.
Manchester, NH: Sophia Institute Press, 1995.

Index

Langham Literature and its imprints are a ministry of Langham Partnership.

Langham Partnership is a global fellowship working in pursuit of the vision God entrusted to its founder John Stott –

> *to facilitate the growth of the church in maturity and Christ-likeness through raising the standards of biblical preaching and teaching.*

Our vision is to see churches in the majority world equipped for mission and growing to maturity in Christ through the ministry of pastors and leaders who believe, teach and live by the Word of God.

Our mission is to strengthen the ministry of the Word of God through:
• nurturing national movements for biblical preaching
• fostering the creation and distribution of evangelical literature
• enhancing evangelical theological education
especially in countries where churches are under-resourced.

Our ministry
Langham Preaching partners with national leaders to nurture indigenous biblical preaching movements for pastors and lay preachers all around the world. With the support of a team of trainers from many countries, a multi-level programme of seminars provides practical training, and is followed by a programme for training local facilitators. Local preachers' groups and national and regional networks ensure continuity and ongoing development, seeking to build vigorous movements committed to Bible exposition.

Langham Literature provides majority world preachers, scholars and seminary libraries with evangelical books and electronic resources through publishing and distribution, grants and discounts. The programme also fosters the creation of indigenous evangelical books in many languages, through writer's grants, strengthening local evangelical publishing houses, and investment in major regional literature projects, such as one volume Bible commentaries like *The Africa Bible Commentary* and *The South Asia Bible Commentary*.

Langham Scholars provides financial support for evangelical doctoral students from the majority world so that, when they return home, they may train pastors and other Christian leaders with sound, biblical and theological teaching. This programme equips those who equip others. Langham Scholars also works in partnership with majority world seminaries in strengthening evangelical theological education. A growing number of Langham Scholars study in high quality doctoral programmes in the majority world itself. As well as teaching the next generation of pastors, graduated Langham Scholars exercise significant influence through their writing and leadership.

To learn more about Langham Partnership and the work we do visit **langham.org**

Lightning Source UK Ltd.
Milton Keynes UK
UKHW020736190519
342860UK00006B/356/P